Ireland

D1061836

A Little History of
IRISH FOOD

A Little History of
IRISH FOOD

REGINA SEXTON

KYLE CATHIE LIMITED

To Alan Davidson –
an inspiration, a guide and a friend

ACKNOWLEDGMENTS

I would like to offer a special word of thanks to all those people who assisted with the
preparation of this book, particularly my parents, Olly and Brigid. Thanks too to
Myrtle Allen, for her ice cream recipe; to Barnaby Blacker; to Simon and Patrick
O'Flynn and Vincent Osborne. Thanks also to Ina Buckley, Denis Hyland, Rory Lehane
and Molly Mannix. More thanks to Kyle Cathie and especially to Kate Oldfield who
edited the text with everlasting patience. But the biggest thanks of all must go to my
husband Shane who is, as always, good enough to eat.

First published in Great Britain in 1998 by
Kyle Cathie Limited
20 Vauxhall Bridge Road
London SW1V 2SA

ISBN 1 85626 243 X

Designed by Prue Bucknall
Home Economy by Marie Ange Lapierre
Edited by David Grant and Kate Oldfield

Printed and bound in Singapore by Kyodo Printing Co (S'Pore) Pte Ltd

CONTENTS

PREFACE

In this very short history, I have endeavoured to identify something of the culture of Irish food, from the rich bank of Irish literary and historical sources. Additionally, the impressively long-lived and often untapped oral tradition has provided some wonderful down-to-earth and unfussy accounts of food, its preparation and people's heartfelt attitudes to the subject in general. Accordingly, the choice of recipes is based to some extent on these findings: items like William Wilde's Potato Fritters, for example, are based on solid historical description; others, notably Mad Sweeney's Soufflé, are playful creations inspired by literary allusion; some, I think of Yellowman Ice Cream, are attempts to use traditional ingredients in a new and exciting manner. Of course, the old reliables, such as Irish Stew, Oatcakes and the variety of potato dishes, dishes which are internationally recognised as typically Irish, have again found voice in this exposition of Irish food. One interesting matter, which is at present diversifying the nature of Irish cuisine, is the re-emergence and resurgence of traditional foods that have over time faded from consciousness, due to a variety of complex cultural developments – I refer particularly to Irish wild foods, venison and the cheese-making tradition in this respect.

While this book does include recipes, its overriding objective is to set

6

Irish food in its unique cultural context. It goes without saying that food cannot be viewed in isolation from culture, and the foods we eat, and the ways in which we prepare them, are products of our cultural identity, and say just as much about us as our language, our music and general disposition. Over the millennia, food in Ireland has done much more than simply nourish the body; it has through time soaked up mythological and folk belief, inspired song and verse, dictated the pattern of our working day and helped us celebrate the myriad of religious and secular festivals. In many ways, therefore, an understanding of our traditional foods provides us with a concentrated insight into who we are and how we got there.

It is of great importance, therefore. to recognise what is truly traditional in an Irish context. Sadly, the study of Irish food has not been given the respect it deserves and the existing record of food traditions has created a less than comprehensive patchwork. With the best intentions, there has been a tendency to use historical archives selectively to avoid certain foods and preparation techniques which might be considered too simplistic or naive to warrant serious attention.

A broader-minded study of Irish food reveals more truths. It acknowledges that many of our foods are simple and peasant in origin. Much is the legacy of poverty and harsh economic circumstances. This small study takes heed of the existence of many other traditions that are the products of a complex history of conquest and colonisation. It also recognises regional food patterns because, I believe, it is crucial to represent Irish food truthfully, not as we might prefer it to be.

What follows does not in the slightest way pretend to be definitive. It merely dips into the rich diversity of material to present a sampling taste of Ireland's past. It owes much to an enormous number of people who surrendered their nostalgic memories of past food traditions to me with honest sincerity. I am happy that they too have found a very important place in this little history of Irish food.

I hope that this collection of historical reference, anecdote and recipes will go some way to deepen the appreciation of Irish food culture.

7

SOUPS & BROTH

*Son of soft rich pottage
with its curls of steam,
son of sprouty meat-soup
with its purple berries.* [1]

It is fitting that this little history of Irish food should start with the subject of soups and broths because they have always had an important part in the Irish diet. Food in Ireland has always been characterised by an impressive abundance of wholesome, fresh and earthy produce. A skillful hand could transform this array into hearty meals, using the simplest and most rudimentary cooking techniques and utensils – the pot, or 'bastible' oven, the baking griddle and, most importantly, the open cauldron which simmered constantly over the open fire. The cauldron inspired Irish cooks to devise endless pottage varieties and soups. Coastal communities gathered up cockles, clams, mussels, oysters, limpets and periwinkles and, adding seaweeds, made up salty soups of the sea. Farmers sat down to meat broths and creamy vegetable soups, while the wonderful foods of the wild, notably nettles, watercress and mushrooms, were free to all who had the mind to style a soupy meal.

It is worth remembering that early medieval soups were first cousins to porridges and gruels. A simple cereal-based preparation, maybe of oats and hot milk or cream, was easily promoted to the rank of soup through the liberal addition of meats and vegetables or whatever was to hand. Indeed, one of Ireland's leading Celtic deities, the Dagda, savoured as his favourite food, a dish which cannot decide whether it is a cereal or a soup. The Dagda is Ireland's greatest mythological gourmand and of his mighty cauldron, we are told, that 'no company ever went away unsatisfied'. On one occasion, the Dagda's enemies, conjure up for him what must be one of Ireland's earliest soup recipes.

8

They filled for him the king's cauldron, which was five fists deep,
and poured four score gallons of new milk and the same quantity
of meal and fat into it. They put goats and sheep and swine into it,
and boiled them all together with the porridge. Then they poured
it into a hole in the ground, and Indech said to him that he would
be killed unless he consumed it all. 2

With the coming of the Anglo-Normans to Ireland in 1169, the cultivation of pulses increased considerably under their influence, especially around the fine arable lands of the south-east. And from this time onwards, peas and beans became available as reputable soup bases and thickeners. In the same fashion, the establishment of great Irish country houses, with their extensive kitchen gardens, in the late-seventeenth and eighteenth centuries, broadened even further the diversity of ingredients available for soup-making. Accordingly, sophisticated soup-making utensils, hitherto unknown or rarely used, became standard kitchen equipment in many of the 'big houses' that grew up all over the Irish landscape. By the early eighteenth century, many estate and large house inventories list the following soup items as commonplace: 'pewter soop plats', 'copper soupe potts', 'silver soup ladles', 'soup tureens', 'sives for peas soape', and 'broth bowls'.

However, the mere mention of soup in an Irish context is often enough to evoke memories of the Great Famine of 1845–9. In February 1847, The Temporary Relief Act, or 'Soup Kitchen Act', was implemented by the British government in an attempt to feed the ever-increasing multitudes of starving Irish. Following the earlier success of various charitable groups in providing soup for the famine stricken, Alexis Soyer, the flamboyant French chef at the famous Reform Club in London, was invited to Dublin, at the request of the Lord Lieutenant, to install soup boilers. Soyer's soup kitchen was opened on the 5th of April 1847 at the Royal Barracks in Dublin.

It was a wooden building, about 40 feet long and 30 feet wide,
with a door at each end; in the centre was a 300 gallon soup
boiler, and a hundred bowls, to which spoons were attached by

9

chains, were let into long tables. The people assembled outside the building, and were first admitted to a narrow passage, a hundred at a time; a bell rang, they were let in, drank their soup, received a portion of bread, and left by the other door. The bowls were rinsed, the bell rang again, and another hundred were admitted. 3

The scheme had limited success. For one thing Soyer's soup recipes typically composed of a quarter pound of inferior quality beef, two onions and other vegetables, half a pound of pearl barley, half a pound of poor flour, two ounces of dripping, three ounces of salt and half an ounce of brown sugar made up to two gallons, was little more than flavoured water and many of those who took it complained of intestinal problems as a result.

IRISH FARM BROTH

When James Boyle recorded his *Ordnance Survey Memoirs* for the parish of Ballymartin, County Antrim in 1838, he drew attention to the tempting hearty broths served up in Irish country kitchens:

The food of the farmers is plain, wholesome and substantial, consisting of fried bacon or hung beef, boiled beef (chiefly in broth). Excellent broth made of beef, groats and oatmeal, leeks and cabbage is a favourite and comfortable dish. 4

Broths not only cheered the soul after a long labouring day, but they were also part and parcel of most country fairs and markets. One observer of the Clogher Fair in County Tyrone remarked in the early 1830s that on fair day the 'people amuse themselves by stuffing themselves with mutton and mutton broth'. Of course the love of meat broths stemmed from the fact that meat, in particular fresh meat, was a rare luxury in the diet of most classes, and so when it came tenderised in its own juices with vegetables, the indulgence was all the sweeter. In some households, where money was tight, sheep's head broths, bulked out with plenty of vegetables and handfuls of pearl barley, were popular. Often, after the family had devoured the soup, the children would retrieve the sheep's skull, scrub it in cold water and parade around the streets with their new macabre toy to the envy of all their playmates.

One sheep's head that made it onto the streets of Dublin was that belonging to the playwright Brendan Behan's grandmother. In his short story 'The Confirmation Suit' he recalls the day that his grandmother cooked up for the first time sheep's head broth:

When she took it out of the pot, and laid it on the plate, she and I sat looking at it, in fear and trembling. It was bad enough going into the pot, but with the soup streaming from its eyes, and its big teeth clenched in a very bad temper, it would put the heart crossways in you. My grandmother asked me, in a whisper, if I ever thought sheep could look so vindictive, but it was more like the head of an old man, and would I for God's sake take it up and throw it out of the window. The sheep kept glaring at us, but I came the far side of it, and rushed over to the window and threw it out in a flash. My grandmother had to drink a Baby Power whiskey, for she wasn't the better of herself. 5

But regardless of this scandalously bad press, I've chosen an excellent meat broth based closely on the great Florence Irwin's recipe from her 1937 publication *Irish Country Recipes*, and note there's not a sheep's head in sight!

Serves 4–6

175G (6OZ) SPLIT PEAS

700G (1½LBS) STEWING BEEF OR LEAN MUTTON

1.7–2.3 LITRES (3–4 PINTS) BEEF OR MUTTON STOCK OR WATER

175G (6OZ) PEARL BARLEY

2 LEEKS

1 CARROT

1 SMALL TURNIP

2 STICKS CELERY

SALT AND FRESHLY GROUND BLACK PEPPER

Soak the peas in water overnight.

Trim the meat of excess fat then place the meat and stock in a large, heavy bottomed pan. Drain the peas and add them and pearl barley to the meat. Cover and cook slowly over a low heat. Wash and peel the vegetables and cut them into bite-size chunks. Add to the cooking pan and season to taste, and cover. Bring to the boil and simmer gently for 2–3 hours, or until the meat is tender.

Before serving skim the fat from the surface with a metal spoon and adjust the seasoning. Then remove the meat and cut into small chunks. Place the meat in individual bowls and ladle over the vegetables and broth. Serve with crusty bread.

Florence Irwin adds: *'To serve country fashion. A pot of potatoes was in readiness. The meat was removed from the pot and cut in small pieces and distributed round the plates, to which the broth was added. In this 2 or 3 peeled potatoes were broken up, and all was eaten with a spoon, the whole forming a warm and substantial meal.'* [6]

CLAM AND COCKLE SOUP

In coastal areas shellfish of any sort was always a welcome addition to the table especially on meatless Holy days, when basketloads of freshly gathered stocks were simply boiled in sea water or in creamy sweet fresh milk. The following recipe is merely an adaptation of these traditional coastal cooking methods.

Serves 6

24 CLAMS

24 COCKLES

ENOUGH WATER TO COVER THE BASE OF EACH SHELLFISH IN THE PAN

40G (1½OZ) BUTTER

1 SMALL ONION OR SHALLOT, CHOPPED

1 STICK OF CELERY, CHOPPED

40G (1½OZ) PLAIN FLOUR

570ML (1 PINT) MILK

110ML (4FL OZ) DOUBLE CREAM

55G (2OZ) CHOPPED CHIVES

Salt and freshly ground black pepper

Wash and scrub the clams and cockles under cold running water, discarding any with broken shells or those that do not close when tapped. Place the clams in one pan and the cockles in another. Cover and steam the shellfish in the water for 5 minutes until the shells have opened. Again, discard any that have failed to open. Strain the cooking liquid of both pots through muslin and reserve. Shell the clams and cockles.In a saucepan melt the butter and sauté the onion and the celery. Blend in the flour, add the clam and cockle broth and the milk and cook for a couple of minutes until the liquids are well blended. Add the cream, stir in the chopped chives and season to taste.

Simmer gently for 10 minutes, add the shellfish, and cook gently for another 2 minutes. Serve immediately piping hot.

FISH & SHELLFISH

Then I saw the doorkeeper, with his tunic of corned beef, and his girdle of salmon skin around him. [1]

A rthur Young, the English agronomist and travel writer, who travelled throughout Ireland in the late eighteenth century, is just one of many outside commentators who has pointed enviously to the wealth of fish and shellfish in Irish coastal and inland waters.

> *The Shannon adds not a little to the convenience and agreeableness of a residence so near it. Besides affording these sorts of wild fowl, the quantity and size of its fish are amazing. Pike swarm in it, and rise in weight to 50lb. In the little flat spaces on its banks are small but deep lochs, which are covered in winter and in floods; when the river withdraws, it leaves plenty of fish in them, which are caught to put into stews... I had also the pleasure of seeing a fisherman bring three trouts, weighing 14lb, and sell them for six pence halfpenny a piece. Perch swarm; they appeared in the river for the first time about ten years ago, in such plenty that the poor lived on them. Bream of 6lb eels are very plentiful. There are many gillaroos in the river, one of 12lb weight was sent to Mr. Jenkinson Johnstown, [on the shores of Lough Derg, Co. Clare].* [2]

But plentiful as these resources may be, the Irish, even to this day, enjoy a somewhat indifferent relationship with fish. Granted, in coastal regions fish was, and still is, a popular player in the diet. However, the gusto with which it is consumed around the coast and in island communities, is unmatched farther inland. Truly a conundrum of gigantic proportions! Is it because fish, in the Irish psyche, is inextricably linked with austere days of

14

religious fasting? Is it because, in some areas, fish was a plentiful free resource and, therefore, classed as a second-rate substitute for meat, acquired only with hard-earned cash? Or is it that the potato was so dominant that it excluded other nourishing foods and, therefore, whole sections of society were denied the opportunity of nurturing a love for the fruits of the river, sea and lake. No doubt these and many other reasons account for this great Irish culinary paradox.

Nonetheless, selective or regional as the exploitation of fish and shellfish may be, it does boast a decidedly fine historical pedigree; and a walk around the Irish coastline will demonstrate its antiquity. Dotted around the coast are hundreds of shell middens, many of them legacies of Ireland's earliest culinary activities. Many of these waste shell deposits are the remnants of Mesolithic or Middle Stone Age (7000–4000BC) food gathering activities. During this period, nomadic groups combed the coastline for shellfish, in particular oysters, mussels, limpets and periwinkles. On some sites, beach-rolled stones, interpreted as limpet hammers, are prevalent. While at one site in Ferriter's Cove, County Kerry a prevalence of small periwinkle shells of uniform size seems to indicate that the younger shellfish were deliberately selected possibly for their sweetness. Evidence that Irish taste buds have been millennia in training! On the estuaries and farther inland, contemporary communities fished for salmon, trout, sea bass and flounder. And there are hints that some of these earliest Irish settlers may have been smoke-preserving salmon for winter use.

Not surprisingly, then, Ireland's well-stocked rivers and seas drew comment and compliment from settlers and tourists alike. One of the first was Giraldus Cambrensis, Gerald of Wales, who came to Ireland in the wake of the Anglo-Norman invasion. In his twelfth-century *Topographia Hibernica (History and Topography of Ireland)*, he writes:

This Ireland is also specially remarkable for a great number of beautiful lakes, abounding in fish and surpassing in size those of other countries I have visited. The rivers and lakes also are plentifully stored with the sorts of fish peculiar to these waters and especially three species – salmon, trout and muddy eels and oily shad. [3]

Later, an anonymous traveller to Ireland gives this more expansive account of the country's riverine and coastal delights. Writing in the late 1670s he states:

> The countrey is water'd by many excellent rivers and rivulets, which are furnished with great numbers of variety of fish... Their seas round about supply them with all manner of shell-fish, and other sorts, the choicest which ever came to Neptune's table. [4]

Others, with a more inquisitive eye, note not only the prevalence of fish and shellfish, but also describe Irish cooking methods. The French nobleman, Charles Étienne Coquebert de Montbret, on his travels around the Kinsale region of County Cork in 1790s, encountered a family grilling their catch of mackerel and mussels over live coals. Besides mackerel, the family had also landed gurnet and pollack. The entire repast, taken with roasted red potatoes, was washed down with grog. Grilled fresh mussels and mackerel and roast potatoes, delicious! With luck, and welcome, others could abandon the role of cool observer and join in the tasty proceedings. In 1841, a number of travellers to the west coast of County Clare were afforded such an opportunity when they decided to stay overnight in a lodging house in Kilkee. Here, after a dubious start, they were fed, watered and entertained;

> preparations were begun for a substantial tea 'à la fourchette'. The waiter, whose heavy-nailed brogues seemed better suited to trampling over a ploughed field than a boarded floor, appeared with a gigantic teapot, and a phalanx of cups and saucers. Then came a broiled red gurnet, and a haddock, an immense pyramid of eggs, and such a dish of smoking potatoes that the bread and butter were quite put out of countenance. Our appetites were in excellent order, and the broiled gurnet soon appeared despoiled of everything save his enormous head and bare back-bone. Our clever friend who had sung the bravura did the honours of the huge teapot right merrily... When the things were cleared away he dashed into an opera; and once begun, gave us the gems and

choice bits of Auber, Bellini, Rossini, Beethoven, one after another,
until we hardly knew whether most to admire his skill, or wonder
at his memory. 5

However, away from the coastal fringes, fish most usually make an appearance on Irish plates during the fast days of Wednesday and Friday. In addition, the vigils of many Holy days and of course the long forty days of Lent were observed as non-meat eating periods. By consequence, fish-eating was regarded as a penitential rather than enjoyable affair. These sentiments were further compounded by the fact that most fish consumed on these days were of the heavily salted stockfish variety, that demanded a long soaking and boiling before it was rendered edible. This was routinely taken with a simple white sauce, *príáil*, of flour, milk, butter and onions. Amhlaoibh Uí Shúileabháin's opinion of salted fish expressed in his dairy on 2 April 1831... 'I do not like salt fish, and fresh fish was not to be had, except too dear and seldom' is an important one and may be taken as widespread. 6 Indeed, a whole generation of Irish people can still recall not only the disagreeable taste of fast-day salt fish, but also the lingering smells of boiling that wafted through the house for the duration of the day. But it wasn't that all fish was considered undesirable. As Amhlaoibh points out: fresh fish was sought after but difficult to access and since a lot of peoples' economic resources afforded them only the salted kind, this tended to taint their relationship, or preconception of fish in general.

In coastal regions the fast days were passed more stylishly, afforded by the custom of consuming bulks of shellfish alongside fresh fish on religious days of abstinence. Good Friday, in particular, saw the tables sway under the burden of their gatherings, when both adult and child sat down to meals of shellfish and seaweeds. And given the community's adventurous and skilful exploitation of resources, the diversity of shellfish gathered to the hearth was immense. William Hamilton Maxwell in his 1892 *Wild Sports of the West of Ireland* outlines the scale in his description of the peasantry on the west coast:

A crowd of a more youthful description of the peasantry are
collected every spring-tide to gather cockles... The quantities of

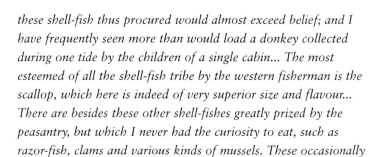

*these shell-fish thus procured would almost exceed belief; and I
have frequently seen more than would load a donkey collected
during one tide by the children of a single cabin... The most
esteemed of all the shell-fish tribe by the western fisherman is the
scallop, which here is indeed of very superior size and flavour...
There are besides these other shell-fishes greatly prized by the
peasantry, but which I never had the curiosity to eat, such as
razor-fish, clams and various kinds of mussels. These occasionally
make a welcome change in the otherwise unvarying potato diet.* 7

For children, shellfish were generally boiled in milk to suit their more
delicate palates. They were also obliged, to ensure good health, to take at
least three meals of shellfish throughout the month of March, possibly to
keep them safe against the harsh March winds. However, despite the
quality and richness of the coastal offerings, communities were often shy
with strangers in promoting their traditional fare, and I have heard of one
story from the 1940s where an inland worker stationed for some time on
the Kerry coast had his landlady stand over him uttering apologies as she
served him scallops fresh from the sea fried in butter, saying it was all they
had for the time being.

But shellfish also had wider functional and protective properties. On
the west coast of Ireland, it was customary each St Brigid's Day (the 1st of
February) to place a live periwinkle or limpet in each of the four corners of
the house, to protect the fishermen and to bring them fishing luck and
plenty for the forthcoming season. This ritual often coincided with the
spring tide when wrack was furiously gathered up to manure the fields as
the new year of agricultural activity was set to begin. Ground-up shell was
highly valued for its lime content and was, therefore, spread on the lands
and potato ridges in areas of acidic soil. Ground-up shell was often mixed
with sand for plastering purposes, while scallops also had a secondary
function, with scallop shell lamps common in many houses.

Irish waters are home to exceptionally fine lobsters which traditionally
have been prized both at home and abroad. One mid-eighteenth-century
account of the Rosses in County Donegal, for example, tells us that lobsters
were abundantly available to all who wanted them and specimens weighing

anything from five to twelve pounds were commonplace. In former times, many were simply lifted by hand or with an iron hook from the rock pools in which they lay, and the folklorist Estyn Evans recalls similar acts of bravery amongst the Kerry lobster catchers. He describes their methods as follows: 'In County Kerry one man would hold another under water with an oar while he searches the holes.' [8] But it was probably the good prices commanded for the lobster farther inland that fuelled such daring acts. Indeed many coastal communities supplemented their otherwise meagre incomes through lobster sales. The eighteenth-century household accounts of the wealthy Carew family, who ran estates in both Waterford and Wexford, illustrate the thriving business in lobster sales between coastal regions and the more affluent buyers living some distance from the shore. On three separate occasions from May to June 1777, lobsters, along with crabs, shrimps and fresh fish, were delivered to their estate in County Wexford. But while the Carews' lobsters didn't have that far to travel from the coast, others travelled far greater distances inland and abroad, thereby making them an expensive luxury sought after by the wealthier sectors of society. As a consequence, lobsters rarely appeared on the plates of those who caught them, and only when prices were low or sales poor did the fishermen sample the product of their hard work.

WILLIAM THACKERAY'S HOT LOBSTER

One unusual method of preparation comes from the pen of the novelist William Makepeace Thackeray (1811–63), who journeyed through Ireland in 1842, publishing an account of his travels the following year as *The Irish Sketch Book*. In this he included what must have been his own favourite recipe for 'hot lobster', which he may have picked up in Ireland:

> *You take a lobster, about three feet long, if possible, remove the shell, cut or break the flesh of the fish in pieces not too small. Some one else*

meanwhile makes a mixture of mustard, vinegar, catsup, and lots of cayenne pepper. You produce a machine called a dispatcher, which has a spirit-lamp under it that is usually illuminated with whiskey. The lobster, the sauce, and nearly half a pound of butter are placed in the dispatcher, which is immediately closed. When boiling, the mixture is stirred up, the lobster being sure to heave about in the pan in a convulsive manner, while it emits a remarkably rich and agreeable odour through the apartment. A glass and a half of sherry is now thrown into the pan, and the contents served out hot, and eaten by the company. Porter is commonly drunk, and whiskey-punch afterwards, and the dish is fit for an emperor. [9]

POTTED SMOKED MACKEREL

In late July or early autumn, when the sun throws dancing diamonds on the sea, the silvery, metallic sheen of the mackerel shoals, giddy for the taste of

sprats, wash and break in swarms against the coast. So swelled are their numbers that any net, or class of container trailed in the water, is guaranteed to bring up fish in great numbers. Those fortunate enough to live beside the coast can, if they choose, live on a mackerel diet until well into November. I have an uncle in Kerry, John O'Leary, who is besotted with the taste of autumn mackerel, and each year, once fresh stocks are running low, he stations a large barrel of cured fish beside the back door to supply his every meal. Traditionally, curing mackerel in brine was the most widespread means of saving the fish into the late year. The fish might equally be hung up to smoke in the open chimney to be preserved by the smoke from the turf fire. It might be nice to try and preserve the smoky taste of this ever-popular fish by potting it to make a type of mackerel pâté.

20

Serves 6

275G (10OZ) SMOKED MACKEREL

75G (3OZ) BUTTER

1 WHOLE SPRING ONION (SCALLION), CHOPPED

1 SMALL CLOVE OF GARLIC, CRUSHED

2 TABLESPOONS FENNEL SPRIGS, CHOPPED

JUICE OF 1 LEMON

SALT AND FRESHLY GROUND BLACK PEPPER TO TASTE

CLARIFIED BUTTER *(see below)*

Skin and bone the mackerel and chop roughly. Soften the butter and cut it into cubes. Place the butter and mackerel in a bowl and blend for a couple of minutes with a fork to form a coarse paste. Add the spring onion, garlic, fennel and lemon juice and continue to blend to a smooth paste. Season to taste.

Place in individual pots and seal with clarified butter. Cover the pots with aluminium foil and store them in the fridge for up to 1 week.

CLARIFIED BUTTER

225G (8OZ) BUTTER

Chop the butter into cubes and place in a saucepan over a low heat until it has melted. Let it settle for 2–3 minutes. You'll notice that the butter has separated into three layers; a white foamy one on top, a rich yellow layer, and a creamy bottom layer of sediment. Once the layers have settled, remove or skim the white surface foam with a large spoon. Slowly pour the yellow liquid from the pan into a waiting bowl, leaving the milky sediment layer behind. Warm this liquid slightly in a clean pan and pour immediately over the top of the little pots of mackerel. Remember, the more butter poured on, the better the seal.

21

POACHED SALMON WITH BUTTERY FENNEL SAUCE

'*Sláinte an bhradáin*', 'the health of the salmon', is the expression used in Ireland when wishing someone well, and indeed it can be demonstrated that the agile and kingly salmon is the most respected and revered fish in the country. This is true in many other countries also, but in Ireland the salmon is so enshrined in our mythology and folklore, that there is a very strong case for making it one of our national emblems.

One story, which recounts how the salmon was granted its wonderful leap, details how St Finian was walking by a riverbank one day and the salmon, seeing the saint, made a gigantic leap from the river into his arms and offered himself as food. Finian recognised the generosity of the deed but declined and instead blessed the fish saying that he and all like him would be blessed with a magnificent leap from that day forward. Likewise, perhaps the best known legend in Ireland recounts how the great hero-seer Fionn Mac Cumhaill achieved his great wisdom by inadvertently burning his thumb on the flesh of the celebrated salmon of knowledge, while cooking for the druid Finnéigeas. Fionn put his thumb in his mouth to cool it down and obtained wisdom: a sure confirmation of the adage that 'fish is good for the brain'.

Salmon is so highly prized and revered in Ireland that it is rarely eaten, it is usually reserved for occasions of entertaining visitors or festivity. The manner of preparation is usually to bake or poach the fish, while historically there were many different methods employed. One common and simple method, if a little impractical in today's typical kitchen, is recorded by the travelling Bishop, Dr Pococke in his *Tour of Ireland in 1752*. When visiting the Giant's Causeway in County Antrim, he notes:

> *I went to the Causeway late, and Mr. Duncane came and dined*
> *with me, and sent a fresh salmon which was roasted before the*

turf fire, it was cut in pieces and stuck on five or six sticks set in the ground round the fire and sometimes taken up and turn'd. [10]

The Reverend Mr S. Hole Reynolds, on his visit to the lakes of Killarney in the 1880s, comes across a similar preparation on one of the islands:

Here, before a glowing fire, a fresh caught salmon, cut into steaks was broiled on arbutus skivers. [11]

This is a well-known recipe for poached salmon in a wonderful buttery fennel sauce.

Serves 12–15

1 LARGE SALMON (FRESHLY CAUGHT, IF POSSIBLE) APPROX.
3.5–4.5KG/8–10LB

For the poaching liquid:

1.4–2 LITRES (2½–3 PINTS) WATER
SALT AND FRESHLY GROUND BLACK PEPPER
1–2 TABLESPOONS FENNEL SPRIGS, FINELY CHOPPED
55ML (2FL OZ) LEMON JUICE

BUTTERY FENNEL SAUCE

250ML (8FL OZ) POACHING LIQUID
250ML (8FL OZ) WHITE WINE
1 LARGE ONION
2 TABLESPOONS DOUBLE CREAM
450G (1LB) BUTTER, CHILLED AND CUT INTO SMALL CUBES
2–3 TABLESPOONS FENNEL SPRIGS, FINELY CHOPPED
SALT AND WHITE PEPPER TO TASTE

Make up the poaching liquid and bring to the boil. Simmer for 15 minutes and leave to cool.

Gut the salmon if necessary and place in a long fish poacher and add enough of the cold poaching liquid to just cover the fish. (Don't use hot liquid as it will cause the skin to break up.) Place the poacher on the stove, bring to the boil and simmer until cooked. Cooking time is generally 8–10 minutes per 450g (1lb). About 10 minutes before cooking is finished, turn off the stove and let the fish cook in its own heat. The fish should feel firm to the touch but should be easily pierced with a skewer.

Make the sauce just before serving. Chop the onion finely and bring to the boil in the poaching liquid and the wine in a heavy bottomed pan. Remove from the heat and add the cream and bring back to the boil. Return to a low heat and slowly add the cold butter, piece by piece. This stage needs patience but it is a crucial stage. At all times the saucepan should only just be warm. To be sure of this hold the pan slightly above the heat. When all the butter is combined, bring the sauce just back to the boil, whisking constantly. Remove from the heat and whisk in the chopped fennel. Season to taste.

Peel the skin from the central portion of the salmon, leaving the head and tail end in place and decorate with wisps of fennel. Serve with the sauce and boiled potatoes. If you are lucky enough to be able to get hold of some rock samphire, it is the ideal accompaniment.

OYSTERS

In the late 1770s, writing of Westpost in County Galway, Arthur Young wrote that one shilling would buy a cartload of oysters. Heaven! William Hamilton Maxwell was also struck by the prodigious numbers off the west coast. Writing in the late nineteenth century he claims that,

> The oysters found in the bays and estuaries along this coast are of very superior quality, and their quantity may be inferred from the fact that, on the shores where they are bedded, a turf-basket large enough to contain six or seven hundred can be filled for a sixpence. A couple of men will easily, and in a few hours, lift a horse-load... [12]

Opposite: OYSTERS

To this day, the fine quality of native Irish oysters is hard to beat, and they are still one of the country's most famous and favourite foods. I think oysters are best enjoyed fresh in their raw state. In many ways, to treat them in any other fashion is to gild the lily. Fresh from the sea, they call out to be eaten in this way; they are self-equipped little packages, providing their own exquisite juice in a natural shell cup.

Allow 6–12 oysters per person
You will also need some lemon wedges.

Pick over the oysters and rinse clean. If you are right handed, cover your left hand in a folded tea-towel and rest the shell lengthways and flat side uppermost in the palm of the hand, making sure your grip is solid and steady (and vice versa if you are left handed). Now take a short oyster knife in the other hand and insert the blade into the shell hinge. Push carefully but with a good pressure and, once the knife is well in, give a sharp twist to prise the shell open, being careful not to spill the oyster liquor. Cut the muscle free from the upper shell and carefully drain this with the juices into the lower one. Slip the knife under the meat to loosen the muscle in the lower shell. Arrange on chilled plates and decorate with wedges of lemon. In Ireland fresh oysters are usually served with buttered wholemeal bread and a pint of stout, but I think that stout is often too heavy an accompaniment and a glass of cool white wine, such as a good Italian Verdicchio, may be a better complement.

Opposite: DE VALERA'S PIE
(see page 30)

BEEF

Corned Beef, my son, whose mantle shines over a big tail Beef-lard, my steed, an excellent stallion. [1]

Lebor na hUidre, or *The Book of the Dun* Cow is one of Ireland's most valued extant manuscripts, dating from the late eleventh century. The naming of the manuscript is a curious one, and if we are to believe the legend, then this book began life as the pet cow of St Ciarán of Clonmacnoise, in County Offaly. When Ciarán was leaving home to begin his tenure at the monastery, his mother refused his request of a cow from the family herd, but the saint was not to be disappointed and one cow strayed from the rest following the saint to the monastery, where she lived as his pet, supplying the milk needs of the monastic community. When she died, it's reputed that her hide was partly used to produce the vellum for *Lebor na hUidre*. Coincidentally, this manuscript contains one of the earliest versions of Ireland's famous epic, *Táin Bó Cuailnge (The Cattle Raid of Cooley)*, a tale well-known to every Irish school child, which centres on the acquisition, by force, of the Brown Bull of Cooley, by Medb, the Queen of Connaught. In short, cows, cows and more cows have pervaded the Irish psyche since at least the early medieval period and, not surprisingly, they have been prized for their sweet and succulent meat as well as their dairy produce. Indeed, since the early modern period, Irish beef has been enjoyed not only at home but throughout Europe and America, and it even filled the bellies of the British Navy throughout the Napoleonic wars. It seems likely then that Beef Wellington could well have started out as a piece of tender Irish fillet!

It wasn't until relatively recently, however, that prime cuts of beef became familiar to a wide Irish audience. Until well into the twentieth

26

century, prime beef was a luxury reserved for Sundays, for special meals of celebration and of course for Christmas, when it joined with the goose as the traditional fare of the season. Ordinary week-days saw cheap beef cuts, offal pieces and salted beef on the table. A glance at any of the manuscript receipt books of the eighteenth, nineteenth and early twentieth centuries will reveal a creative use of stewing beef and the careful utilisation of every scrap of the Sunday joint, which was most often recycled into Monday's tasty Shepherd's Pie. Accordingly, many of these older recipes, familiar to our mothers and grandmothers, like Exeter Stew with dumplings, Sea Pie (reworked below as De Valera's Pie), Mince Collops, Rissoles, Boiled Beef, Stewed Ox-Tail, and Stuffed Bullock's Heart have now bowed out of the weekly family menu because the re-use of meat and cheaper cuts is no longer considered acceptable in a society which is affluent enough to buy fresh meat on a daily basis.

One outstanding factor which militated against the consumption of beef, at least in the early medieval period (AD500–1200), was the size of one's cattle herd. In the heavily stratified society that was early Ireland, the extent of the cattle herd was an indication of social status. Thus, maintaining the herd and augmenting it was of constant concern, and as a by-product, cattle-raiding was a riotous, regular and accepted feature of society. *The Annals of Ulster*, for example, record for the year 1031 the following highly successful raid by the Ulstermen into the north-east region of the province

> *Eochaid's son led an expedition to Telach Óc and achieved*
> *nothing. Aed ua Néill passed round him eastwards and took away*
> *three thousand cows and twelve hundred captives.* [2]

In particular, the newly inaugurated king was socially obliged to execute the royal cattle-raid (*creach rígh*), to demonstrate his potential as an effective and confidence-inspiring leader.

In a society where cattle were highly visible indicators of social status, it was customary to keep herds of milch cows primarily for their dairy produce, therefore making beef a highly prized food, reserved for the aristocratic families. The authoritative scholar on the cattle economy of

early Ireland, the late Dr A. T. Lucas, has this to say about the state of affairs: 'the overwhelming bulk of the cattle population consisted of cows… a herd of bullocks would have been an unthinkable phenomenon and so it is to be suspected that all bull calves were killed at birth.' [3] If we accept this argument, then it is highly likely that throughout the calving season veal would have been a prominent part of the diet amongst farmers with substantial herds. Despite Lucas' argument, it is also probable that small herds of bullocks were kept especially to stock the aristocratic tables – as seems to be verified by the Irish legal texts which demanded that yearling and two-year-old bullocks be surrendered as part of the food rents exchanged between farmers and their lords. What is more, the fact that these laws demanded sturdy, healthy and well-fattened animals, suggests that cattle were carefully reared to a high quality standard:

> A calf of the value of a sack, eight hands in girth, sound after
> being made a bullock, which grazes along with the milch cows,
> whose two haunches reach his two kidneys, except the breadth of
> three fingers, not killed by fairy plague or other diseases, but
> slaughtered by the person by whom it was reared… [4]

It also seems that many yearlings were fed a high milk and grain diet to maximise meat flavour. The following description of a calf destined for the feast of the noble Bricriu is an important one in this respect in that it points to a specialised fattening programme to produce first grade marbled flesh:

> a fine beeve… from when it was a little calf neither heather nor
> foigdech [some plant or shrub] entered its mouth but full new milk
> and liugfér [possibly new-mown grass] of green grass and corn. [5]

When everyone finally got around to eating the meat, the laws of this intensely hierarchical society dictated the cut proper to each grade:

> the haunch for the king, bishop and literary scholar; a leg for
> the young chief, the heads for the charioteers and a steak for
> the queen. [6]

Throughout the sixteenth and seventeenth centuries, various Tudor and Stuart writers, many working as Crown agents, cast a somewhat jaundiced eye on the great cattle herds of the Gaelic Irish and their strange meat-eating habits. Fynes Moryson, Secretary to the Lord Deputy, Lord Mountjoy, writing in his *Itinerary* (1617), paints this over-simplified, though interesting picture of the Irish cattle economy:

> *This plenty of grass, makes the Irish have infinite multitudes of cattle, and in the heat of a last rebellion, the very vagabond rebels had great multitudes of cows, which they still (like the nomads) drove with them, whithersoever themselves were driven, and fought for them as for their altars and families.* [7]

Some time earlier, Edmund Campion, in his *Two Bokes of the History of Ireland* (1570) is one of many to point to the absence of bread and the high quantities of beef consumed, often in a half-raw state:

> *They drink whey, milk and beef-broth. Flesh they devour without bread.* [8]

We must, however, take these findings with a very large grain of salt. Gaelic aristocratic families enjoyed a varied diet, of which spit-roasted 'beeves' were a popular and frequent part and, outside these circles, beef was most frequently consumed salted, prepared in the same manner as salted bacon.

Indeed, corned or salted beef was to emerge as one of the country's largest export products by the end of the seventeenth century. The emergence of the Irish Provision Trade, where huge quantities of salted beef, butter and, to a lesser extent, bacon were exported throughout the British Empire, came as a direct result of the imposition of the Cattle Acts of 1663 and 1666, when Irish exports of live cattle were severely penalised and eventually banned. Cork, in particular, became one of the leading beef curing and slaughtering centres in the British Isles. By 1776, Cork City was exporting 109,052 barrels of salted beef annually to ports in England, Europe, and even as far away as the West Indies and Newfoundland, consequently earning for itself the titles 'the slaughterhouse of Ireland' and 'the ox-slaying City of Cork'. Such developments effected a marked increase in beef consumption, especially amongst the wealthier sectors of Cork society, while the poor were left with copious quantities of the coarser offal cuts. Arthur Young, for example, notes that Cork cellar or slaughterhouse workers were supplied with seven pounds of offal per week to help feed their families. And of course, the slaughterhouses with their waste blood by-products were to create that well-known unique Cork delicacy, drisheen – Cork's own pure beef and sheep blood pudding.

Far from Irish shores, Irish corned beef was used as a secret weapon in the ongoing disputes between the British and the French. Lord Chief Baron Edward Willes gives this interesting account of the destination of Irish beef in the mid-eighteenth century:

> *I had the curiosity to enquire how they dispose of all parts of the ox slaughtered for exportation, and was informed, they had two methods of doing it. If it was for the merchants' service, the whole beef, neck as well as other coarse pieces, were all barrel'd up together, but if for the English Navy, the necks and coarser pieces were not put into the barrel. They have a third sort which they call French beef, that is old cows and beeves that are but half fat, which in time of peace they sell to the French. This sort of beef turns black and flabby, and almost to a jelly (no wonder sailors fed with this meat can't face our honest English Tars, who have so much better and more substantial food in their bellies).* [9]

DE VALERA'S PIE

In the 1930s, the Fianna Fáil Government under the leadership of Eamon de Valera issued a number of cookery books designed for use by young girls working under various schemes run by the Department of Agriculture.

In terms of presentation, these are stark and mundane publications, products of their time, outlining the basic principles of good cooking. Nonetheless, the list of recipes is impressive, covering everything from Kedgeree to Rabbit Pie to Roly Poly Puddings, and these were carefully crafted to suit even the most modest income. Some time ago, I had the privilege of inspecting one such book in close detail, after a neighbour, Molly Mannix, kindly offered me her grandmother's much used 1936 edition. Delighted, I thumbed through the recipe pages and read with glee advertisements for the 'New Series of Powered Agas', model 62, price £62. But then I noticed a suspect advertisement 'To All Unmarried Students' submitted by a Dublin butcher who boasted:

> during a quarter of a century, [we have] earned the gratitude of a host of housewives who, before marriage, looked forward with eager anticipation to donning an apron and 'attempting' the perfection their cooking exhibits to-day. [10]

In other words, all young girls aspire to the married state and within this station their cooking talents will prosper. Interestingly, this dogma also reappeared in another government publication, Eamon de Valera's 1937 Irish Constitution, Bunreacht na hÉireann, where Article 41 2.1 tells us:

> In particular the State recognises that by her life within the home, woman gives to the State a support without which the common good cannot be achieved. [11]

and 2.2:

> The State shall, therefore, endeavour to ensure that mothers shall not be obliged by economic necessity to engage in labour to the neglect of their duties in the home. [12]

Nowadays many people find these sentiments offensive, since they may be seen to convey the idea that a woman's place is in the home, where she will presumably cook away to her heart's content, maybe using her 1930s government cook book, until her hungry husband comes home. In salute to

all those kitchen-bound Free State women, I've adapted one almost forgotten beef stew recipe, cooked with a soda bread crust, from the 1936 book. Here it's given the curious name 'Sea Pie' which was originally a pie not of seafood but of meat, vegetables and potatoes, baked with a suet pastry lid. The name arose because it was often served at sea to sailors. I have, however, substitued a soda bread crust, and for devilment I've enlivened it with liberal amounts of good Irish stout.

To make this dish you need to prepare the stew first then cook it in a warm oven for 2– 2½ hours. For the last 30 minutes or so of cooking, the soda bread dough is added as a lid which will bake away into a crusty topping (see photograph opposite page 25).

Serves 4–6

900G (2LB) LEAN STEWING BEEF, CUT INTO GENEROUS CHUNKS

2 TABLESPOONS PLAIN FLOUR, SEASONED WITH SALT AND PEPPER TO TASTE

3 TABLESPOON VEGETABLE OIL

I LARGE ONION

I CLOVE GARLIC, CRUSHED

225G (8OZ) SWEDE TURNIP

225G (8OZ) CARROTS

340ML (12FL OZ) STOUT

I BUNCH FRESH THYME, FINELY CHOPPED

Preheat the oven to 160°C/325°F/gas mark 3.

Trim the meat of excess fat and toss it in the seasoned flour until lightly coated.

Heat the oil in a wide pan, and throw in the meat and move around until well browned. Remove the meat with a perforated spoon and place in a casserole (for this recipe a round casserole is preferable, as the finished dish with a round cake of soda bread looks much more effective).

Prepare and chop the vegetables. Add the onions and garlic to the pan and cook for a few minutes until soft and transluscent. Remove and transfer to the casserole. Cover the base of the pan with 3–4 tablespoons of stout, bring to the boil, stirring all the

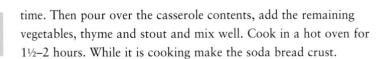

time. Then pour over the casserole contents, add the remaining vegetables, thyme and stout and mix well. Cook in a hot oven for 1½–2 hours. While it is cooking make the soda bread crust.

SODA BREAD CRUST

(Double the measurements to produce a conventional soda bread,
working to the instructions below – see recipe on page 92)
225G (8OZ) PLAIN FLOUR
½ TEASPOON SALT
½ TEASPOON BICARBONATE OF SODA (BREAD SODA)
150ML (6FL OZ) BUTTERMILK

Sieve all the dry ingredients into a bowl, mixing well. Make a well in the centre and pour in most of the buttermilk. Then, working around the bowl, draw the flour into the buttermilk, continuing in this circular fashion until all has been absorbed. When the dough comes together it should feel sticky but pliable. If you feel the dough needs a little more moisture add the remaining buttermilk. Turn onto a floured board, kneading lightly, giving it just one or two turns to fix into shape.

With the palm of your hand pat the dough out into a circular cake (of about 1cm/½in thickness) to the circumference of the casserole. With a cake of such thinness it will cook well and not remain stodgy on the under surface. Alternatively, follow Dorothy Hartley's advice for preparing a 'Sea Pie' lid in her authoratative work, *Food in England* in which she suggests cutting the dough to shape by pressing the casserole lid into the rolled surface of the dough. Remove the casserole from the oven and lift the soda bread carefully on top of the stew, making sure that it covers the surface of the simmering meat. Score the surface deeply into four. Dust the surface with a light coat of flour and replace the casserole lid. Turn up the oven heat to 200°C/400°F/gas mark 6 and bake for 30– 40 minutes.

When cooked cut through the four quarters of soda bread crust

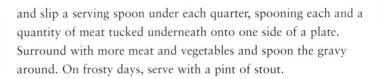

and slip a serving spoon under each quarter, spooning each and a quantity of meat tucked underneath onto one side of a plate. Surround with more meat and vegetables and spoon the gravy around. On frosty days, serve with a pint of stout.

SPICED OX TONGUE

In the weeks coming up to Christmas, butchers' shops all over Ireland offer for sale strange-looking logs and rounds of beef, smothered in coats of powdered pimento. This is spiced beef, an Irish Christmas speciality.

I suspect that spiced beef was a regular visitor to the tables of the aristocracy from the later medieval period. One Hiberno-English poem, *The Land of Cokaygne*, preserved in a fourteenth-century manuscript, refers to an expansive array of spices that would delight the modern-day cook. Candied ginger, galingale, mace, cinnamon and powdered cloves are mentioned alongside spiced beef:

> *The meat is spiced, the drink is clear,*
> *No raisin-wine or dull slops there!* [13]

However, in Cork, spiced beef is available all year round, but at Christmas time some butchers also throw a few ox tongues into the spicing barrel. So in place of beef, I'm giving a recipe for spiced tongue. It was provided for me by my husband who, when young, and with his mother, prepared ox tongue on a regular basis. Cold tongue is an ideal snack or picnic food.

Serves 4

For the spice mixture: enough to spice an average
tongue of about 1.25kg/3lbs

6 TEASPOONS POWDERED ALLSPICE

4 TEASPOONS POWDERED BLACK PEPPER

3 TEASPOONS POWDERED CLOVES

1 TEASPOON POWDERED GINGER

50G (2OZ) DRY JUNIPER BERRIES (THESE ARE SOFT, CRUSH THEM BY HAND IF YOU WISH)

I TEASPOON POWDERED MACE

I TEASPOON POWDERED NUTMEG

3 BAY LEAVES, CRUSHED

I ONION, FINELY MINCED

A FEW PINCHES FRESH THYME, FINELY CHOPPED

25G (8OZ) COARSE SALT

340G (12OZ) SOFT BROWN SUGAR

10G (½OZ) SALTPETRE (AVAILABLE FROM MOST CHEMISTS)

To simmer with the tongue:

I ONION, STUCK WITH SOME CLOVES

2 CARROTS

I SMALL TURNIP

2 SPRIGS OF THYME

I SMALL BUNCH PARSLEY

2 BAY LEAVES

FRESHLY GROUND BLACK PEPPER

Combine the dried spices in a pestle and mortar. Then, in a bowl, mix them with the minced onion and add the fresh thyme, salt, sugar and saltpetre and mix well.

Thoroughly rub the spice all over the tongue and place in a large earthenware dish. Cover and place the bowl in a fridge or cold place for 10–14 days, rubbing in the spice and turning the tongue once a day. The longer the tongue is left in the spice, the stronger the flavour will be.

When ready, simply place the tongue in a deep pan of cold water, to which you can add the vegetables, herbs and pepper. Bring to the boil and simmer for 2–3 hours until cooked. The tongue is ready when it feels tender when tested with a skewer.

Remove from the water and let it cool for about 5–10 minutes. While still warm, skin the tongue and, as an alternative to rolling and pressing it, fix it lengthways on a board, skewering both ends with two large forks. When cold the forks can be removed and the tongue will remain in this long shape, enabling it to be carved at right angles.

LAMB & MUTTON

Haunch of Mutton
Is my hound's name, Of lovely leaps.
Lard, my woman, Sweetly smiles
Across the top of kale. [1]

Traditionally in Ireland, most sheep herds were kept for their wool, milk and milky white cheeses, and so when sheepmeat reached the table it was usually in the form of mutton, taken only when the animal had spent its productive years. By consequence, lamb and fattened young wethers were considered a delicacy from early medieval times, and were demanded as food rents by the aristocratic classes. Sometimes, if a young animal died through misadventure, then lamb featured as an unexpected treat on the plates of the small to middling farmer. Even as late as the nineteenth century, the prospect of tasting roast lamb was greeted with great glee and even merriment. In her memories of rural Ireland in the late nineteenth century, Mary O'Brien recalls the day a young sheep died by accident and the resultant excitement to get it on the spit as soon as possible:

> 'there's roast lamb for our dinner... the crayther! fallin' from the rocks the way it did to break its neck, and it neither a lamb nor a sheep. With mint sauce it is lamb,' I said firmly. 'Make a good fire and have it on the spit in plenty of time....and then run to the eel-stream for a double-handful of mint.' [2]

Not surprisingly, then, given that the economic value of sheep lay in their secondary produce, the killing of an animal to entertain a surprise guest was the sign of genuine hospitality. The English traveller, The Reverend Dr Richard Pococke, comments on such an occurrence in his *Tour in Ireland in 1752*:

36

The people in this Country are very hospitable, if you cannot stay to have a sheep killed they offer Ale a dram, Eggs and butter, and the woman of the house sits at the table and serves you. 3

An earlier commentator, Luke Gernon, Second Justice of Munster, was also presented with a fattened wether, by way of welcome, when he visited a castle of the Gaelic aristocracy in the early seventeenth century. Here, after an obligatory tasting of the whole array of house drinks: beer, whiskey, sack and old ale, he chose, from a variety of meat cuts, an unusually prepared dish of 'swelled mutton':

The dish which I make choice of is the swelled mutton, and it is prepared thus. They take a principal wether, and before they kill him, it is fit that he be shorn. Being killed, they singe him in his wooly skin like a bacon and roast him by joints with the skin on, and so serve it to table. They say that it makes the flesh more firm and preserves the fat. I make choice of it to avoid uncleanly dressing. 4

One aspect of the Irish palate, which influenced the preparation of mutton and indeed all meats, was the taste for serving portions of boiled and roasted flesh at the one sitting. When the English bookseller and traveller, John Dunton, called at the home of the comfortable O'Flaghertie family in Connemara in the late 1600s, plates of both roasted and boiled mutton were offered around to impress their guest:

there was a mutton killed for supper, half of which was boyld and the other roasted, and all devour'd at the meale. 5

However, more often, mutton demanded long boiling to render an acceptably tender flesh. Specially designed free-standing low three-legged pots or mutton pots were called into service for the boiling, and if the dish was properly prepared Irish mutton, and in particular mountain mutton, was famed for its quality and sweetness. The County Down-born writer and sportsman, William Hamilton Maxwell, impressed by Irish mountain mutton during his adventures in the west of Ireland in the early nineteenth century, recalls an evening when he 'dined sumptuously from mountain mutton and a fine 'John Dory'. [6] Similarly, in 1841, an anonymous English traveller is equally flattering in his appraisal of succulent mountain mutton reared on the upland slopes of County Clare:

> *The pasture of Bishop's island, as we afterwards learned, is considered the sweetest and most nutritious of any in the country; and the mutton fed upon its hallowed soil is always offered for sale with an extra confidence in its merits... 'an elegant quarther-raal island mutton; as small as anything, as sweet as honey, and that will melt in your mouth.'...there is no where such good mutton as at Kilkee.* [7]

If mutton was not taken fresh, it was salted down for later consumption and until a generation ago, salted mutton continued to enjoy considerable popularity, even though its availability was limited, relative to corned beef and bacon.

IRISH STEW WITH MAIZE DUMPLINGS

To add a carrot or not?, that is the great Irish Stew controversy. Purists denounce any carrot that makes it into the stew as a no-good hanger-on, useless for taste and texture, and there only for personal gain; to bask in

the glory of being associated with Ireland's most famous national dish. Other nefarious characters who vie for a role in the stew include, beef, celery, turnips and pearl barley, although these too are rejected out of hand as non-traditional ingredients. For many a real Irish stew is limited to neck mutton chops or kid, onions and potatoes and indeed these are the only ingredients listed in many of the hand-written Irish receipt books [recipe books] of the eighteenth and nineteenth centuries.

It seems that Irish Stew was recognised as a national dish as early as the eighteenth century and one contemporary English broadsheet ballad is devoted entirely to lauding its merits;

Some like herrings red from the ocean,
And some like a bit of pig's fry;
Some like oxtail soup, I've a notion,
While others like a pudding and pie.
For all sorts of stomachs there are dainties,
But the best feed between I and you,
Is some mutton with onions and potatoes,
Made into a real Irish Stew,
Then hurrah for an Irish Stew,
That will stick to your belly like glue;
The sons of St Patrick for ever,
And three cheers for a real Irish stew. [8]

Traditionally neck mutton pieces or kid was the only meat used in the preparation of this peasant casserole, however, as mutton is increasingly difficult to come across lamb chops or stewing lamb pieces will suffice.

Serves 4
900G (2LB) MUTTON OR LAMB CHOPS (NECK OR SHOULDER CHOPS ARE
    NORMALLY USED)
3–4 MEDIUM SIZED ONIONS
900G (2LB) POTATOES
4 CARROTS (OPTIONAL)
SALT AND FRESHLY GROUND BLACK PEPPER
I HANDFUL CHOPPED PARSLEY
I PINT WATER OR MUTTON STOCK
I GENEROUS SPRIG OF THYME

For the maize dumplings:
55G (2OZ) SELF-RAISING FLOUR
55G (2OZ) FINE MAIZE FLOUR

1 TEASPOON PARSLEY, FINELY CHOPPED

1 TEASPOON THYME, FINELY CHOPPED

PINCH OF SALT

55G (2OZ) BUTTER

1 EGG, BEATEN

A LITTLE COLD WATER AS NECESSARY

Preheat the oven to 180°C/360°F/gas mark 4.

Trim the chops of excess fat and cut each in half. Peel and chop the onions roughly.

Wash and peel the potatoes and cut into rounds or slices of about 5mm (¼in) thickness. If you are using carrots, wash and scrape them and cut them into chunks. Place a layer of meat on the bottom of a deep casserole and cover with a layer of onions and then potatoes (and carrots). Season well and sprinkle with chopped parsley (saving a little for the garnish). Repeat this procedure building up layers until all the meat and vegetables are used up. Pour in the water or stock until the fluid almost reaches the top of the casserole. Add the thyme and bring to the boil on the stove top. As soon as it boils, cover and transfer to the oven and leave to simmer for 2 hours. After the first hour of cooking make sure that there is enough liquid to accommodate the dumplings, if not top up to the right quantity.

To make the dumpling dough sieve the flours into a mixing bowl and combine with the herbs and the salt. Then rub in the butter until the mixture resembles fine breadcrumbs.

Add the beaten egg and mix with enough water to make a sticky, though firm dough. (Be careful not to add too much water. If the dough is too soft the dumplings will not hold their shape.)

With floured hands break the dough into 8–10 pieces and roll in the palms of your hands into little balls. Add to the casserole for the last 30 minutes of cooking time.

To serve, ladle the stew into individual bowls giving each person 2–3 dumplings. Sprinkle with chopped parsley.

ROAST LEG OF LAMB WITH APPLE & MINT JELLY

Lamb, is a relative newcomer to the family of Irish traditional food and up to a few generations ago, and certainly in the more distant past, the thought of butchering a young animal was unheard of given the economic importance of the animal's secondary produce. However, once the taste of young tender lamb, reared near the coast or freely in open pasture was discovered, it immediately won an adoring audience. So much so, that it is now relatively difficult to procure the more traditional mutton, much to the disappointment of the older generation who still long for its stronger taste.

Spring lamb is regularly served as a festive treat to celebrate Easter Sunday, where it is often served with a helping of tasty lap. In Ireland a 'lap of lamb' is the popular term for the long, thin strip of meat and fat that runs from the breast bone of the lamb through to its leg. It can be butchered on or off the bone. When you buy a leg of lamb, many butchers will include the lap free of charge, wrapped around the leg. It can be roasted alongside, underneath or on top of the joint. Many people relish this piece because it is so flavoursome and crispy.

Serves 6

1 LEG OF SPRING OR EARLY SUMMER LAMB WITH A PIECE OF LAP
  (ROUGHLY 2.7KG/6LB, INCLUDING BONE)
3–4 CLOVES GARLIC, PEELED
SALT AND FRESHLY GROUND BLACK PEPPER
Preheat the oven to 200°/400°F/gas mark 6.

Wipe the meat and trim off any excess fat. Chop the garlic lengthways into thin sticks. Then puncture deep holes in the surface of the skin and push in the garlic sticks. Rub the pepper into the skin and sprinkle with a good coat of salt.

Place the lap in a roasting tin and sit the leg on top. Cook in the preheated oven for 20 minutes, reducing to 180°C/350°F/gas mark 4 for the rest of the roasting. Remove the lap from beneath the joint and place it alongside the joint to crisp. Roast for

1–1¼/1½ hours depending on whether you desire your meat to be rare, medium or well-done. Remove the leg joint to a serving plate and keep warm.

Cut the lap into strips (cutting down between each separate little bone if butchered on the bone) and keep warm with the joint while you make the gravy.

½ PINT CHICKEN OR LAMB STOCK IF AVAILABLE

2–3 TABLESPOONS SWEET SHERRY

1 TABLESPOON APPLE JELLY (SEE BELOW)

Skim off the excess fat from the juices in the roasting tin using a metal spoon. Then add the stock and bring to the boil, stirring all the time to dislodge the crispy meat bits. Once boiled, reduce to a simmer and add the sherry and dissolve the jelly through the gravy. Pour into a warm gravy boat and keep in a warm place until ready to serve.

Carve the lamb carefully, giving those who want them a strip or two of crispy lap. Serve with gravy and Apple Mint Jelly (see below), and lots of roast potatoes and a little puréed sorrel dressed in 1–2 tablespoons of double cream.

APPLE OR APPLE & MINT JELLY

Makes 450g (1lb) of jelly

900G (2LB) APPLES (WINDFALLS ARE GOOD)

570ML (1 PINT) WATER

450G (1LB) SUGAR

(2 TABLESPOONS LEMON JUICE FOR APPLE AND MINT JELLY)

(1 BUNCH OF MINT, CHOPPED FINELY FOR APPLE AND MINT JELLY)

Wash and cut the unpeeled apples in half and place in a large, heavy based pan or preserving pan. Pour in enough water from the pint so that the level is just visible below the line of fruit. Bring to the boil and cook until the fruit is softened to a pulp. Remember to stir occasionally to prevent it sticking to the pan. Place in a jelly bag and leave to drip its juice into a container in a cool place for 2 days.

Measure the juice and allow 450g (1lb) sugar for each pint. Return the juice and sugar to the pan. (If you are making Apple & Mint Jelly add the mint and lemon juice and continue as follows.) Bring to the boil, stirring until all the sugar is dissolved. Continue to boil until the setting point is reached.

Pour into warm, sterilised jars and seal with either wax discs or twist-on-lids at once.

A note on setting:
Take a spoon of jelly and drop it onto a clean plate. Leave it for a few minutes. If little ridges appear on the jelly's crust when the jelly is pushed from the side with your finger, it is ready.

PORK

Fair was the shape of that man and his name was Bacon-lad, with his smooth sandals of old bacon, and leggings of potmeat encircling his shins.'[1]

The following words of the well-known Irish novelist and dramatist, John B. Keane, from his wry and witty book on Irish food, *Strong Tea*, are ageless sentiments and would sit well in the Ireland of any age, such was the love of good quality pork and fine homecured hams.

> *Lest the wrong impression be given, let me say at once that the type of bacon I have in mind is homecured. It has been hanging from the ceiling for months, and when you cut a chunk from it there is the faintest of golden tinges about its attractive shapeliness. When this type of bacon is boiling with its old colleague, white cabbage, there is a gurgle from the pot that would tear the heart out of a hungry man.* [2]

Pork, ham and bacon are, without doubt, the most traditional of all Irish foods, featuring in the diet since prehistoric times. Throughout the early medieval period (AD500–1200) wild boars, native to Ireland's once vast tracts of deciduous woodlands, were hunted with great gusto for their delicious flesh, with the best cuts reserved for the warrior classes. Indeed, generous joints of pork, roasted on spits over open fires or boiled in cauldrons, are often central features of many of the early Irish romantic heroic sagas.

The ninth-century tale *Scéla Mucce meic Dathó (The Story of Mac Dathó's Pig)* mentions the seven cauldrons in Mac Dathó's hostel:

> *Each cauldron contained beef and salted pork, and as each man*
> *passed by he thrust the flesh-fork into the cauldron, and what he*
> *brought up is what he ate; if he brought up nothing on the first*
> *try, he got no second chance.* 3

If he was lucky enough to haul out a piece on the first go, then he could be assured of its quality given the attention devoted to the feeding and fattening of both wild and domesticated pigs. In the autumn, boars, pigs and piglets enjoyed the oak mast of the woodlands. So important was this resource, that it is acknowledged by an entry in the *Annals of Clonmacnoise* for the year 1038:

> *There was such an abundance of ackornes this yeare that it*
> *fattened the pigges [runts] of pigges.* 4

In addition to the roaming pigs of the woodland, a select number were kept and intensively fed in and around the farmsteads. Here, the feeding of the pigs was exclusively women's work, and they fattened them up on a mash of milk and corn, thus improving their flesh quality prior to slaughter. So important was the woman's role in this farm activity, that if she decided to divorce her husband, a frequent occurrence in early Ireland, then her work effort was rewarded and she walked away from the union loaded down with her salted flitches of bacon, free to contract a new marital union with any hungry medieval Irish man.

After the slaughter, meat was hard-cured for home use, but the best quality flitches formed part of the food rents paid by farmers who rented cattle fiefs from their local aristocratic lords. Along with beef, wethers, onions, leeks, curds and cheeses, a specifically proportioned piece of pork was also handed over:

> *a pig's belly worth a sack, nine fists in length, a fist with the*
> *thumb extended being the breadth of its fork in front, a fist being*
> *the breadth of its fork behind, three fists being its breadth in the*
> *middle, three fingers its thickness in the middle.* 5

The introduction of the potato to Ireland in the late sixteenth century served as a great boost to the pig economy. In good years, the potato harvests were so bountiful that even the poorest households could afford to keep and fatten one or two pigs on a potato-rich diet. Usually, one pig was fattened as the porker for the home table, while the other fellow was equally important as he was the 'gentleman who paid the rent', sold off at the local pig fair as a valuable source of income. This pig, says the Reverend Mr S. Hole Reynolds, an Englishman who travelled through Ireland in the nineteenth century, 'is precious and he has his privileges'. Taking the tone of the Irish farmer, he adds: 'I think that nobody has a better right to the run of the house, whether up stairs or down stairs, than him that pays the rint' [6]. So plentiful were pigs at this time that on the eve of the Great Famine in 1841, the pig population was calculated to be 1,412,813. Indeed, some time earlier, the English agriculturist, Arthur Young, who travelled through Ireland in the late 1770s, was forced to comment on their enormous numbers. He says that 'hogs are kept in such numbers that the little towns and villages swarm with them; pigs and children bask and roll about, and often resemble each other so much, that it is necessary to look twice before the *human face divine* is confessed' [7]. Of the town of Mitchelstown in County Cork he adds, 'I believe there are more pigs than human beings.' However, the recurrent potato failures in the early nineteenth century left the small farmer and cottier without the necessary surplus potato stocks to fatten his swine. Therefore pig husbandry diminished considerably among the poorer sections of society.

STUFFED ROAST PORK STEAKS WITH BAKED APPLES AND POTATO CAKES

Slaughtering the pig usually took place in late autumn or early winter since pork was viewed with suspicion at any time when there wasn't an 'R' in the month, given that the heat of the summer months caused the meat to turn foul. Since most farms reared at least one pig for home consumption, the days after the slaughter saw a welcome glut of pork products on the table. The hams and ribs were salted down, and some of the larger pieces were taken from the brine barrel after about two weeks, wrapped in brown paper and hung on hooks up the chimney to smoke. Black and white puddings were made up using much of the offal by-products, some were parcelled up in bundles for the neighbours, who in turn returned the favour when they killed their own pig. Heads, tails and feet, if not eaten fresh or salted, were hived off for the manufacture of brawn. But of all the pieces, it was the pork fillet or steak that was relished the most, as this was one of

the few lean pork pieces to be eaten fresh. Ina Buckley grew up in the town of Newmarket in County Cork in the 1940s and she related to me her colourful memories of eating fresh pork steak and pig lard:

> *The steak was delicious and she [my mother] would cook it in the oven, a large wide flat heavy cast-iron cooking pot with a lid, which was normally used for baking bread. She would have onions with it, and it would be fried in the suet from the pig. The suet was put into the oven and rendered over a hot fire to extract the lard. When it was melted, she placed it in large jam jars and kept it for roasting or frying. It was delicious. Sometimes we had fried bread cooked in this lard and I can still remember the flavour of it on a cold frosty morning, before going off to school. Yummy!* [8]

The pork and the apples take 1 hour to bake so they can both be cooked at the same time.

Serves 4

2 x 450g (1lb) pork fillets (called pork steak in Ireland)

For the stuffing:

225g (8oz) breadcrumbs

Salt and freshly ground pepper

1 pinch ground cinnamon

1 large onion, finely chopped

47

75–110G (3–4OZ) BUTTER

1 BUNCH OF FRESH HERBS (E.G. THYME, PARSLEY, CHIVES AND A LITTLE
SAGE), FINELY CHOPPED

100–150ML (4–5FL OZ) CIDER
Preheat the oven to 180°C/350°F/gas mark 4.

Trim the fillets of excess fat. Then cut the fillets open and flatten
gently. This is done by making an incision into each fillet, cutting
down the length and opening the fillet out from the split edges.

To make the stuffing:
Season the breadcrumbs with salt and pepper and add the
cinnamon. Sweat the onion in 25g (1oz) of butter and mix into the
breadcrumbs. Add the herbs. Melt the remaining butter in a heavy
saucepan and pour into the breadcrumb mixture. Season to taste.
Mix well and spoon into one of the pork fillets. Place less stuffing
at the tail ends of the pork, as it may spill out if over-stuffed. Place
the other fillet on top, pressing down gently so that the sides of the
fillets come together to enclose the stuffing. Secure the fillets with
twine, tying at intervals up the length of the meat. As the twine is
tightened the fillets will take on a more cylindrical shape but don't
be over-enthusiastic with the tightening! Secure the tail ends well.

Smear the fillets with butter, place in a casserole and pour over
the cider. Cover with tin foil and cook in the oven for 1 hour,
removing the foil for the final 15 minutes. Drain and reserve the
cooking juices for sauce making.

Snip and remove the twine before carving individual portions.
Serve with the Apple Sauce, Baked Apples (recipes below) and the
Potato Cakes (see page 78).

APPLE SAUCE

55ML (2FL OZ) PORK JUICES (FROM THE COOKING ROAST)
55ML (2FL OZ) CIDER

225G (8OZ) COOKING APPLES, CORED AND SLICED

SUGAR TO TASTE

225G (8FL OZ) WHIPPING OR DOUBLE CREAM

Pour the meat juices and cider into a saucepan, add the apples and sweat over a low heat until the apples become pulpy. Sweeten to taste.

Pureé this mixture in a blender and press through a fine sieve. Return the pureé to a clean saucepan, add the cream and heat gently. Season to taste.

BAKED APPLES

Allow 1 eating apple per person:
To fill 4 apples:
110G (4OZ) UNSALTED BUTTER
2–3 TABLESPOON BROWN SUGAR
1 TEASPOON CINNAMON
1 TEASPOON POWDERED CLOVES
Preheat the oven to 180°/350°F/gas mark 4.

Wash the apples and remove a plug of 1cm/½in diameter from the stalk and bottom ends. Set aside and reserve. Remove the rest of the cores.

In a bowl, combine the butter, sugar and spices to a paste and stuff into the apples. Replace the plugs to seal in the paste. Bake in the oven for 1 hour.

BAKED HAM

The eleventh-century Irish poem *Aislinge meic Conglinne (The Vision of Mac Conglinne)* has the following evocative description of cooking a salt-and honey-seasoned piece of bacon over an open fire. It is interesting to note how the cook expertly manages to seal in all the juices. This picture of a nimble-toed cook, donning his linen hat and apron, must, I believe, be one of the earliest references to specific cooking attire:

49

He called for juicy old bacon, and tender corned-beef, and full-fleshed wether, and honey in a comb, and English salt on a beautiful polished dish of white silver, along with four perfectly straight white hazel spits to support the joints. Then putting a linen apron about him below, and placing a flat linen cap on the crown of his head, he lighted a fair four-ridged, four-apertured, four-cleft fire of ash-wood, without smoke, without fume, without sparks. He stuck a spit into each of the portions, and as quick was he about the spits and fires as a hind about her first fawn... He rubbed the honey and the salt into one piece after another. And big as the pieces were that were before the fire, there dropped not to the ground out of these four pieces as much as would quench a spark of a candle. 9

Serves 4

1.8KG (4LB) JOINT SMOKED HAM

4 TABLESPOONS BREADCRUMBS

4 TABLESPOONS DEMERARA SUGAR

ENOUGH HONEY TO SPREAD OVER THE COOKED JOINT

WHOLE CLOVES FOR BOILING AND STUDDING (OPTIONAL)

Soak the ham in cold water overnight to extract excess salt.

The next day, drain the ham, discard the water and place in a large, heavy based saucepan and cover with cold water. Bring to the boil, if a lot of white scum settles on the surface, this indicates that the salt content is still high so discard the cooking liquid, re-cover the meat with cold water and bring to the boil again. If you desire, throw a good few cloves into the cooking water for added flavour. Simmer steadily, not allowing it to boil, allowing 20 minutes per 450g (1lb) and 15 minutes over.

Opposite:
COLCANNON (see page 66)
and STAMPY (see page 82)

Preheat the oven to 220°C/425°F/gas mark 7.

Once cooked, remove from the pan and set aside to settle and cool slightly for about 5 minutes.

Meanwhile, mix the breadcrumbs into the sugar. Then peel the brown skin and some of the thick fat from the joint (at this point it should come off easily). Rub the honey into the fat and sprinkle on the sugar and breadcrumb mix. (Stud with cloves if you wish.)

Place the joint in a roasting tin and crisp the coating in the oven for 10 minutes. Remove and allow to settle for 10–15 minutes before carving.

The traditional accompaniment to ham in Ireland has always been cabbage, cut up and cooked with the ham for the last 30 minutes, to take on the flavour of the meat. Should you wish to try this, omit the cloves at the boiling stage.

Opposite: APPLE AND RHUBARB
CHARLOTTE (see page 68)

POULTRY & GAME

To the sustance of Lent
–the cock and the hen. [1]

The once extensive deciduous forests of Ireland, together with the rolling scrub and the salty coastal marshes, have always offered a rich supply of game, there for the taking, to all who enjoy the produce of the chase. One anonymous seventeenth-century traveller in Ireland noted:

> *Their marshes and rivers (of which they have plenty) are visited by multitudes of wild fowl in the winter season... their hills are stored with woodcock, grouse, heathcock, etc. Nor are they a little stored with red-deer, hares and rabbits.* [2]

Closer to home, the well-stocked farmyards provided a constant supply of milder fleshed fowl. However, the fact that farmyard birds were easily reared and always close to hand made them a regular feature of Irish plates, in contrast to their more difficult to source wild relatives. Geese and hens in particular have historically been the firm favourites since at least the early medieval period (AD500–1200). Indeed their presence in tremendous numbers may be gleaned from the fact that they are regularly accounted for in the body of early Irish literature and their good looks have also ensured that their attractive plumage has been immortalised in such masterpieces as the famous eighth-to ninth-century gospel book, *The Book of Kells*. Fowl also made it into the literary texts because of their characteristic bad behaviour.

The seventh-to eighth-century legal text, *Bretha Comaithchesa*, ('Judgements of Neighbourhood') refers to the crimes of hens who were prone to repeatedly raiding neighbouring houses and farmyards:

*All the birds are as the hens, with respect to their trespasses...
The three hen-trepasses in a house are snatching away, wasting
and spilling. The three hen-trepasses in an enclosure are soft
swallowing of bees, and injuring roid [a plant cultivated for
dyeing] and onions. Three cakes is the fine for their trepass in a
house, and half a scerpall [a unit of value] in an enclosure or
herb garden and sacks [of grain] are charged upon them outside
the enclosure. 3*

And if they were not deterred by such policing then the legal text stipulates
that they should be condemned to wear rag boots to limit their freedom.

In the wake of the Tudor and Stuart settlements, the turkey made its
appearance in Ireland and like all exotic new food imports, it took some
time to reach the tables of the non-aristocratic classes. By the eighteenth
century, however, the turkey seems to have earned popular appeal,
appearing in the diets of many sectors of society. For example, the wealthy
Carew family of Castleboro, County Wexford purchased 'six couple of
turkys' in July 1752, while some time later in 1795, the less well-to-do
Franciscan Friars of Cork also enjoyed the bird on a regular basis.
Although judging by William Makepeace Thackeray's experience of
turkey-eating in Galway, it is questionable whether or not the flesh
appealed to all palates. Sitting down to dinner at Kilroy's Hotel, he and
four others were presented with two turkeys. Thackeray did the honours of
carving and he continues to relate the story as follows:

*There are, as it is generally known, to two turkeys four wings. Of
the four passengers, one ate no turkey, one had a pinion, another
the remaining part of the wing, and the fourth gentleman took the
other three wings for his share. Does everyone in Galway eat three
wings when there are two turkeys for dinner? 4*

Notwithstanding this mind-boggling event, hens, geese, ducks and turkeys
were widely enjoyed due mainly to the fact that there was little or no
export market for fowl. This, together with the fact that they could be
sustained and well-fattened on surplus potato stocks, made their keeping a

viable concern in the domestic economy. It might be timely here to draw attention to Arthur Young's much-quoted description of an Irish potato meal, where he states that not only did the family enjoy proceedings but also 'the cocks, hens, turkeys, geese, the cur, the cat, and perhaps the cow'. He also offers a more encompassing summary of the economic and social factors which propelled the peasantry towards fowl-rearing:

> *poultry (are) in many parts of the kingdom, especially Leinster, are in such quantities as amazed me, not only cocks and hens, but also geese and turkeys; this owing probably to three circumstances; first, to the plenty of the potatoes with which they are fed; secondly, to the warmth of the cabbins; and thirdly to the great quantity of spontaneous white clover (Trifolium repens) in almost all the fields... upon the seeds of this plant the young poultry rear themselves.* 5

He also points to the fact that many fowl have their legs tied to prevent them trespassing into neighbouring farmers' grounds; a development of the medieval practice referred to above. Indeed, it is safe to say that the half door, a standard feature of the Irish vernacular house, was put in place with the notorious roaming abilities of hens and other fowl in mind. The housewife often maintained her laying hens in the house where, because of the warmth of the kitchen, they continued to lay throughout the year. Whether confined to the house or roaming the open farmyard, the constant company of the hens gave rise to a number of folktales explaining their behaviour. A widely held belief was that hens were brought to Ireland by the Norsemen and, therefore, since they were really outsiders, they secretly harboured hostility towards the Irish. When they were seen scraping at the floor, for example, people surmised that they were attempting to burn the house down. And their banter before bed-time was interpreted as their nightly determination to return in feathery force to their homeland. But, alas after a night of sleep, they awoke oblivious to the previous night of planning and scheming, and so spent their nights repeating the procedure over and over again. Despite all this negativity, hens, throughout the nineteenth and early twentieth centuries, contributed in a very positive

sense to the household economy, when the trade in eggs gave many a housewife much needed pin money to make ends meet. They also became the bartering tools between rural housewives and grocers, who exchanged them for items like tea, sugar, tobacco and white bread, often at much inflated prices.

GOOSE

The vast flocks of free-ranging geese, alluded to in so many of the historical sources, appeared on Irish tables on three special occasions, Michaelmas (the 29th of September), St Martin's Eve (the 11th of November), and of course Christmas Day. The eve and festival of St Michael the Archangel was also celebrated as *Fomhar na nGéan*, the Goose Harvest, or 'the Eve of Michaelmas of the Geese' as Amhlaoibh Uí Shúileabháin (1780–1838), a schoolmaster and shopkeeper from Callan, County Kilkenny, author of the earliest known diary in Ireland, liked to call it. This was the time of year when geese were sufficiently fattened for the market. It was also customary to mark the day with a special goose dinner. Amhlaoibh again, for example, observed the tradition in September 1831. He records in his diary entry for 29th September 1831 that he 'had a dinner – beef and potatoes – for four pence halfpenny...also a share of Michaelmas goose.' [6]

But sitting down to face the goose on St Martin's Eve came after a day of strange ritualistic practices. On this day each year, a farm animal, or more usually a goose or hen, was slaughtered out of doors and, while still bleeding, the bird was rushed indoors where its blood was sprinkled in the four corners of the house; a symbolic gesture enacted in an attempt to gather in luck and fortune for the forthcoming year. Now, if appetites were still sharp after these goings on, the family gathered around the table to a dinner of goose. And indeed, the sharing spirit which gelled small rural communities together made certain that the even the poorest families tasted a piece of fowl on this night; and birds were shared around to make this aspiration a reality. Christmas too brought bastible roasted geese bursting with potato stuffing, and for some days after Christmas, goose in various shapes and forms featured at most meal times. There was, of course, goose soup, giblet soup and gravy, and the curious goose drisheen. This latter dish was a mixture of finely chopped onion, flour, oatmeal, salt and pepper mixed into the collected blood of the slaughtered bird. The mixture was simply left to settle in a bowl, and called goose drisheen.

Roast goose was often served on one other very special occasion in Ireland, and that was usually the day a 'match' between a young couple had been settled. Matchmaking in Ireland was not a light-hearted affair and a successful match-made-marriage was considered to be one between couples of equal social status. For months in advance, matchmakers, sometimes professional and working for a fee, set about bringing the couple together. Once dowry payments had been fixed or more unusually a financial settlement reached when a man married into a farm of land belonging to the woman's father, a trip to the solicitors was made to seal the marriage bargain. More often than not the young married couple continued to live in the family house of the parents, who now officially surrendered the farm and the running of the house to their son or daughter and new in-law. However, the parents still demanded special privileges such as a field for a cow, a seat by the fire and the front seat in the cart going to mass. These concessions, along with financial aspects of the marriage, were thrashed out in town with the solicitor. When all were happy, both sets of parents and the soon-to-be-married couple retired to one of the parental homes, where the successful business was celebrated with a roast goose dinner.

ROAST GOOSE WITH POTATO STUFFING

Serves 8

For the giblet stock:

GOOSE GIBLETS (HEART, NECK AND GIZZARD)

1 ONION

1 CARROT

1 STICK CELERY

1 BOUQUET GARNI (1 SPRIG THYME, 1 BAY LEAF, 1 SMALL BUNCH PARSLEY)

A FEW PEPPERCORNS

A LITTLE COLD WATER AS NECESSARY

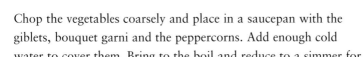

Chop the vegetables coarsely and place in a saucepan with the giblets, bouquet garni and the peppercorns. Add enough cold water to cover them. Bring to the boil and reduce to a simmer for 2 hours. Strain and reserve for the gravy.

For the stuffing:
110G (4OZ) STREAKY BACON, FINELY CHOPPED
1 LARGE ONION, CHOPPED
900G (2LB) POTATOES, BOILED IN THEIR SKINS
75G (3OZ) BUTTER
A LITTLE MILK
1 TABLESPOON FRESH SAGE, CHOPPED
1 TABLESPOON FRESH THYME, CHOPPED
SALT AND FRESHLY GROUND PEPPER

Fry the bacon until crisp and remove from the frying pan with a perforated spoon and reserve. Cook the onions in the bacon fat until they are soft but not browned. Reserve.

Peel the cooked potatoes and mash with the butter and enough milk to render them smooth and lump free. Add the bacon, onion and chopped herbs and mix well. Season to taste with salt and pepper.

To prepare the goose:
1 WELL-HUNG OVEN-READY GOOSE WITH GIBLETS (PREFERABLY A BIRD OF NOT MORE THAN 4.5KG/10LBS; LIGHTER ONES ROAST BEST)
A LITTLE LEMON JUICE
SALT
Preheat the oven to 200°C/400°F/gas mark 6.

Prepare the bird by washing thoroughly both inside and out, pulling away any fat from inside the cavity. Dry well. Rub a little lemon juice into the cavity.

Now stuff the cavity and truss the bird, binding the legs and wings to maintain its shape while cooking. Rub salt into the skin and prick all over with a sharp fork to allow the free flow of excess fat. Sit the goose breast side down on a wire rack in a roasting tin. Roast the goose in the preheated hot oven for the first 30 minutes, then reduce the heat to 160°C/325°F/gas mark 3 and roast for 3–4 hours, depending on the weight of the bird. Geese from 3.5–4.5kg (8–10lbs) need 3–3½ hours; 4.5–5.4kg (10–12lb) need from 3½–4 hours.

Check the bird from time to time, periodically pouring off the fat collected in the roasting tin. (Keep this fat in reserve for future roast potatoes!) Half way through the cooking, turn the bird breast side up. Test for readiness by putting a skewer into the thickest part of the thigh. When the juices run clear you will know that the bird is done.

Once cooked, place the goose on a serving dish reserving the juices in the roasting tin to make the gravy.

To make the gravy, pour off most of the fat from the juices left in the roasting tin, retaining a little to very thinly coat the base of the pan. Blend in 2–3 tablespoons of flour to make a paste. Add 570ml (1 pint) of the giblet stock and bring to the boil, stirring all the time, to loosen the crispy meat bits adhering to the pan base. If the gravy is too thick add a little more stock. Season to taste. Strain and pour into a gravy boat for serving.

VENISON

Among the most commonly found archeological sites in the Irish landscape are the *Fulachta Fiadh* or 'Deer Cooking Pits', which are littered across the countryside. These sites were in use from the early Bronze Age c.1800BC, right through to the seventeenth century, testimony to the fact that the pursuit of game and its culinary preparation has a tremendous antiquity. The consumption of venison has at all times been the preserve of the aristocracy and high ranks of society as early medieval sources confirm. One particularly interesting post-medieval (or possibly earlier) reference relates how a young woman 'Mis', who represents the sovereignty of Ireland, has become mad and deranged and it falls to her young suitor,

Dubh Ruis to pacify and placate her. Following an amorous encounter, he cooks a deer in the cooking pit and uses the hot steam and the grease of the deer to clean and renew her former self. Brian Ó Cuív's translation is as follows:

> *With that he cut the deer's throat and skinned it. Then he made a large fire of dead wood from the forest and he gathered a heap of granite stones, and put them in the fire. He made a pit, square all round in the ground, and he filled it with water. He cut up his meat and wrapped it in marsh grass, with a well-turned sugan [a twisted rope of hay or straw]around it, and he put it in the hole and he was supplying and continuously putting the well-reddened, long-heated stones in the water, and he kept it constantly boiling until his meat was cooked... He then took her to the hole in which was the cold broth with the fat of the deer melted on it, and he put her standing in it, and he took a piece of the deer's skin and he rubbed and massaged the joints of her body and all her bones, and he took to smearing her, rubbing her, and spreading her with the grease of the deer and with the broth until he had cleaned much of her, and until he brought streams of sweat out of her like that.'* [7]

The Anglo-Norman lords, who arrived in Ireland from Pembroke in Wales in the twelfth century, also displayed a passion for the chase. They not only introduced fallow deer into the country, but in the thirteenth century they also developed special fallow deer parklands such as Brestwood, County Dublin and Glencree, County Wicklow to manage the herds and promote the chase.

From the eighteenth century onwards, the systematic management of deer herds and the consumption of venison was maintained as part of the culture of the big house, and one need only glance at the lines of antler trophies that dot the walls of these estate houses to see how integral a tradition it was. Indeed, the many receipt books from the kitchens of these houses invariably give pride of place to dishes such as 'Roast Haunch of Venison', 'Venison Pie', 'Potted Venison' and 'Venison Pasties'. In recent years, deer farming has grown into a very successful enterprise and this often elusive meat is now available for all to indulge in.

ROAST SADDLE OF VENISON WITH CRABAPPLE AND SLOE JELLY

Most recipes for venison suggest marinating the meat before cooking. This is often necessary because the venison can be dry and tough, if not tasteless. However, if you have a competent butcher, who slaughters the deer at the right age, hangs it for the correct period of time and advises you on the best cuts, the marinating process is no longer necessary. The most important consideration in the following recipe is keeping the venison from drying out.

Serves 8

2.4KG (5LB) SADDLE OF VENISON (THE SADDLE IS SUPERIOR TO THE
   HAUNCH WHICH IS MUCH DRIER)

SALT AND FRESHLY GROUND BLACK PEPPER TO TASTE

STREAKY BACON (ENOUGH TO COVER THE SADDLE)

1 HEAPED TABLESPOON JUNIPER BERRIES

2 GLASSES RED WINE

110G (4OZ) BUTTER

Preheat the oven to 200°C/400°F/gas mark 6.

Rub the salt and freshly ground pepper into the saddle of venison. Then cover the saddle with the streaky rashers, keeping them in place with some cooking twine if necessary.

Place in a large, close-fitting casserole with the juniper berries and 1 glass of red wine. Melt the butter in a saucepan and pour over the saddle. Cover the casserole and place in the preheated oven for 10 minutes per 450g/1lb, or 15 minutes for a more well-done joint.

During the cooking, continue to baste the meat with the butter and add the second glass of wine as the other reduces. For the final 20 minutes, remove the lid from the casserole to brown the joint. Remove the meat from the casserole and allow to settle in a warm place while you make the gravy.

¾–1 PINT BEEF OR GAME STOCK

5FL OZ RED WINE OR PORT

1 TABLESPOON JUNIPER BERRIES, LIGHTLY CRUSHED

2 TEASPOONS CORNFLOUR DISSOLVED IN 2 TABLESPOONS WATER

SALT AND FRESHLY GROUND BLACK PEPPER, TO TASTE

Skim the fat (if any) from the roasting tin with a metal spoon. Add the stock, wine/port and the juniper berries to the remaining juices in the roasting tin. Simmer over a moderate heat for 5 minutes, stirring constantly. Remove from the heat and leave to and thicken the sauce by slowly bringing to the boil, again stirring all the time. Season to taste and transfer to a warmed gravy boat while you carve the meat.

Serve the roast venison with fluffy mashed potatoes and some sautéed mushrooms. The unique, tarty taste of Crabapple and Sloe Jelly makes it an ideal accompaniment.

CRABAPPLE AND SLOE JELLY

You will need to make this well in advance, when the sloes and crabs are ripe during the months of September and October.

Makes approximately 450g (1lb) jelly

450G (1LB) SLOES

450G (1LB) CRABAPPLES

570ML (1 PINT) WATER

450G (1LB) SUGAR (APPROXIMATELY)

Wash the fruit. Cut the crabapples in half and place in a large saucepan with the sloes and mix together. Proceed as outlined in the recipe for Apple Jelly (page 42).

FRUIT & VEGETABLES

A row of fragrant apple-trees
An orchard in its pint-tipped bloom
A forest tall of leeks
Of onions and of carrots stood . [1]

In the very early sixth-century BC Greek text, *Massiliot Periplus*, Ireland is described as being 'rich in turf among the waves and thickly populated by the *Hierni*'. This term, known officially as '(H)ierne' is a version of the Celtic *Iwernyu*, whence Irish *Éiru, Éire*, 'Ireland' are derived. And what is of interest here is that linguistic scholars can demonstrate that the root of this word means 'fat' and 'fruitful'. The case is plain. Ireland is well named: a land of fat fruitful bounty, a most fertile and bountiful country, whose rich soils have long supported prodigious crops of fruit and vegetables.

The earliest historical sources in Ireland abound with references to the fertility of the land. In the saga literature which relates tales of the Kings of Ireland, their successful reigns are mirrored by bountiful harvests of fruit and vegetables.

From scant references, it is possible to identify some of the vegetables that were cultivated in early Ireland. In one seventh- to eighth-century law tract, *Bretha Crólige* or 'the Law of Sick Maintenance', which details correct procedures for care of the sick, there is reference to the *Lubgort* (a herb or vegetable garden), in which grow a number of vegetables conducive to good health. Two particular vegetables alluded to are *fír-cainneann* and *imus*. The first of these, *cainneann*, is generally taken to be an allium and has been variously translated as onion, garlic or leek. Its prefix *fír*, usually translated as 'fresh', may equally be taken to mean that which has been cultivated in a garden, as opposed to varieties that might be gathered from the wild. Whatever its true identity, it seems that some member of the

allium family (stalk, bulb and clove) was eaten regularly and often salted and pickled for winter use.

Imus, the other vegetable mentioned above, is regularly rendered as 'celery' or 'parsley', and while these are reasonable guesses, they cannot be taken as definitive. In any case *imus* seems to be a vegetable that is juicy, mild on the stomach and generally good for convalescing invalids, perhaps even a vegetable broth!

In the body of hagiographical literature relating to Irish saints, we see that St Ciarán of Saigher dined every evening on a small bit of barley cake, taken with two *mecons* or root vegetables, grown in the enclosed monastic garden. Again the reference here seems to be to cultivated roots such as carrots or parsnips rather than to wild roots such as burdock. We also know that various brassicas were cultivated in Ireland as the penitential monks treated themselves on days of festival to a condiment of kale with their otherwise sparse allowance of dry bread.

Of early cultivated fruits, apples are the most prevalent, and references to them abound. One, well-known to most Irish schoolchildren who are read the great Irish Celtic saga tales in primary school, makes use of apples in a description of the great Irish hero Cúchulainn during his spasm of rage:

> The warp-spasm seized Cúchulainn, and made him into a monstrous thing, hideous and shapeless, unheard of. His body made a furious twist inside, so that his feet and shins and knees switched to the rear and his heels and calves switched to the front. The hair of his head twisted by the tangle of a red thornbush stuck in a gap; if a royal apple tree with all its kingly fruit were shaken above him, scarce an apple would reach the ground but each would be spiked on a bristle of his hair as it stood up on his scalp with rage. [2]

Of course, a host of wild fruits also brought a decided sweetness to the diet, and allusions to the collecting of blackberries, wild raspberries and strawberries, myrtle and whortleberries (see page 116) are common. Incidentally, blackberries were also used as eye-shadow by the missionary monks who darkened their eyelids with juice. Sloes were also abundant, and in the *Annals of the Four Masters*, we are informed that the year 1031 was so fertile that hundreds of black-red sloes could be bought for a penny. The inherent bitterness of sloes and crabapples could be softened by cooking them down with mellow honey.

However, it was the successive waves of colonisers and outside settlers we must thank for diversifying the Irish fruit and vegetable diet. The Anglo-Normans, for example, who first arrived in Ireland in 1169, greatly influenced the increased cultivation of peas and beans, in particular in the eastern regions, areas of high Anglo-Norman settlement. Accordingly pease and bean pottages were supped up with bits of 'maslin' breads, made from mixed cereal flours. In harsh times, especially when the cereal crops were poor, peas and beans were ground to meal and used in the preparation of emergency style breads.

The developed tastes of the Anglo-Norman lords provided a new tradition of gardening in Ireland. Dr Charles Nelson of the National Botanic Gardens points out that by the end of the fourteenth century a scribe from County Kildare recorded a poem attributed to one Master Jon Gardener, which provides the earliest work on gardening in the English language.

> All of the herbys o Ierlonde
> Here thow schalt ham knowe eueri onde. 3

It gives us a lengthy list of the types of vegetables possibly found in Ireland, including 'spinage, lettuce, radish' and herbs such as 'thyme, rue, sage' and 'savory'. 4

The great diversity of vegetables cultivated by the upper classes is also clear from the details of the various types of herbs and vegetables available to the fellows of Trinity College Dublin from the seventeenth century. Dr Nelson's study reveals that in 1605 'turnip, parsnip, carrot, artichoke, onions, leeks and cabbages were cultivated in the college gardens. By 1683 the college also cultivated parsley, lettuce, corn salad, winter cole, thyme and peas. 5

While one sector of society enjoyed the ever-increasing diversity of vegetables, the potato came to dominate the diet of the poor. In the 1770s,

Arthur Young commented on the lack of vegetable cultivation 'neither pease, beans, nor rape in the country, but turneps and clover are creeping in among the gentlemen'. [6] Later he indicates that the turnip was grown essentially as animal fodder.

Most cottiers had a cabbage plot. This is very much true today and I would venture to say that after the potato, cabbage must be considered Ireland's favourite vegetable. Today, alongside nearly every rural household in the country, vivid green patches made up of proud clusters of rounded cabbage plants are to be seen. Acquaintances of mine have been known to telephone their wives from work to request that they might put down, not one, but two heads of cabbage for the dinner. The cabbage is traditionally boiled in the salty water provided by the accompanying piece of hairy bacon, or pig's head, or half dozen crubeens (pigs' feet), or, on occasion, the cushion of ham. Cabbage must be recognised as one of the indispensable ingredients of what might be classed the most archetypal of all Irish meals. Amhlaoibh Uí Shúileabháin (see page 55), a schoolteacher and draper from Callan, County Kilkenny, records such a meal in his diary entry for the 19th of July 1827, when he goes with some friends to visit the farmland of Mr Power:

> We got a good dinner from Mr. Power, namely, fat smoked swine flesh, that is, bacon, white cabbage, magnificent potatoes and hot-mixed whiskey or punch. We came home leisurely and in a cheerful mood. [7]

A well-known dish which combines both cabbage and potatoes is Colcannon. The earliest reference to this most traditional of dishes that I have come across dates to 1735 and comes from the diary of William Bulkely from Bryndda on Anglesey in Wales. During a sojourn in Dublin, he notes down the supper he had on Hallowe'en:

> 31st. Dined at Cos. Wm. Parry, and also supped there upon a shoulder of mutton roasted and what they call there Coel Callen, which is cabbage boiled, potatoes and parsnips, all of this mixed together. They eat well enough, and is a Dish always had in this Kingdom on this night. Apples, nuts, ale, &c., after supper. [8]

COLCANNON

The familiar tradition that new-born babies are found in the cabbage patch is well established in Ireland, but the cabbage in Ireland has even more superstitious and interesting features. One tradition is observed at Hallowe'en (the 31st of October), when young girls blindfold themselves, head out into the cabbage patch and lift a cabbage of their choice. They then examine the nature of the root of the cabbage plant and its characteristics, long, short, hairy, dirty and so on, and these qualities are taken as portends of their future husbands. The same cabbage is taken in and boiled up, to be combined with potatoes to offer the traditional dish of Colcannon, which is in turn used to continue the process of foretelling. A ring is concealed in the large bowl of Colcannon, which is placed in the centre of the gathered assembly who, armed with spoons, consume it feverishly in an effort to procure the ring: whoever does so will be next to marry. An allied tradition involves young girls placing the first and last spoons of Colcannon into one of their stockings, which they then hang on the back of the door. The first man through the door is taken to be their future husband. The following is my favourite Colcannon recipe and, as well as its being ideally suited to foretelling one's future spouse, it is a wonderful addition to any meal. (See photograph opposite p50.)

Serves 6–8

900G (2½–3LB) LARGE, FLOURY POTATOES (GOLDEN WONDERS OR KERR'S PINKS ARE GOOD)

1 SPRING OR SAVOY CABBAGE

4–5 LARGE SPRING ONIONS (SCALLIONS)

150ML (6FL OZ) WHIPPING CREAM

LIBERAL QUANTITIES OF BUTTER

FRESHLY GROUND BLACK PEPPER

Wash the potatoes and boil them in their skins (which really does result in a superior flavour). While they are boiling, wash the cabbage and cut it into quarters. Remove the hard core and cut finely across the grain. Cover the bottom of the pot with about 1cm (½in) of salted water (or ham stock if at hand) and add the cabbage. Boil until soft and then drain. Add some butter and some black pepper.

Once the potatoes are cooked and have been left to dry, remove their skins. Chop the spring onions and sweat for a little while in some melted butter. At the same time, heat the cream in a saucepan until quite warm, being careful not to boil. Mash the potatoes, slowly adding enough of the heated cream to make the potatoes soft and fluffy. Add to the cabbage and onions and mix thoroughly. As a rough guide, the potato and cabbage should be in equal proportions.

Serve in a large bowl and don't forget to serve with little 'lakes' of melted butter on top, as specified in the well-known pre-cholesterol song:

Did you ever eat colcannon,
When 'twas made with yellow cream
And the Kale and Praties blended
Like a picture in a dream?
Did you ever scoop a hole on top
To hold the melting lake
Of the clover-flavoured butter
That your mother used to make? [9]

FRUIT

Apart from apples, pears and soft berry fruits, the greatest variety of fruit was cultivated in the walled gardens of the large aristocratic estates. Here, considerable care and attention was devoted to nurturing exotic fruits for the table. Many fruits were imported specifically for this purpose. In December 1683 for example, among other trees, Sir John Percival imported thirty-six peach and nectarine, eighteen fig, thirty

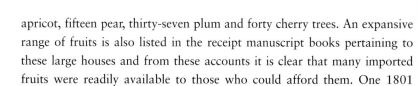

apricot, fifteen pear, thirty-seven plum and forty cherry trees. An expansive range of fruits is also listed in the receipt manuscript books pertaining to these large houses and from these accounts it is clear that many imported fruits were readily available to those who could afford them. One 1801 manuscript from County Waterford includes recipes for the following dishes prepared from imported (or possibly home-grown, non-native) fruits:

> *Lemon Puddings, Orange stuff for torts, Gooseberry wine,*
> *Currant Wine, Plumbe Pudding, Raspberry Vinager, China Orange*
> *Jelly and so on.* [10]

It is interesting to note that, with the emergence of the independent farming class in the late nineteenth and early twentieth centuries, a major expression of their new-found confidence was the planting of small orchards and soft fruit bushes, mirroring the culture of the Big House. This is still very much the case today, and many rural households will have a dozen apple trees and a cluster of blackcurrant and gooseberry bushes.

In an urban context, Ireland has always enjoyed a lively importation trade of the more exotic species. A regular pastime for young Cork children was the fortnightly journey down to the quays to look at the 'Banana Boat' and, if lucky, to come away with a long bunch of green bananas, to be ripened in the hot press. Shop windows were full of the wonders of preserved fruit, crystallised oranges, lemons and greengages in addition to the undulating layers of figs, prunes, apricots and dates. A number of years back, when a young courting couple went to the pictures (cinema), the onus was on the young man to produce a small oblong box of dates, complete with long fork, which was taken as the chief token of good taste and guaranteed to capture the young lady's fancy.

APPLE AND RHUBARB CHARLOTTE

This recipe combines the homeliness of bread and butter pudding, the stickiness of caramel and the refreshing taste of sweetened tart fruit, all smothered in cream (see photograph opposite page 51). I have adapted a recipe from Margaret Bates' publication, *The Belfast Cookery Book*, 1967.

Serves 4

175G (6OZ) BUTTER

1 TABLESPOON WATER

350G (¾LB) APPLES (SMALL COX'S PIPPINS OR BRAMLEYS)

350G (¾LB) RHUBARB AND BLACKBERRIES, MIXED

55G (2OZ) SOFT BROWN SUGAR

2 TEASPOONS GOLDEN SYRUP TO SWEETEN

1 EGG YOLK, BEATEN

55G (2OZ) CASTER SUGAR

1 LOAF WHITE BREAD, THINLY SLICED

CASTER SUGAR FOR DUSTING

Preheat the oven to 220°C/425°F/gas mark 7.

Melt 1 tablespoon of butter with 1 tablespoon of water in a saucepan. Peel and chop the fruit into chunks and add it to the saucepan too. Cook gently until the fruit is soft. Add the sugar and syrup and taste. Add more sugar if necessary. When the fruit has cooled a little, add the beaten egg yolk and mix well.

Butter a charlotte mould (or a 1.2-litre/2-pint pyrex bowl, if you haven't one) and dust liberally with the caster sugar. Melt the remaining butter. Remove the crusts from the bread and cut into 3cm- (1Gin-) wide fingers. They should be as long as the depth of the mould. Dip each in melted butter and use to line the sides, making sure that each finger overlaps the next slightly.

Cut 2 circles of bread exactly the same size as the top and bottom of the mould. Dip both in melted butter and put the round for the crown of the mould in position. (At this point, you can seal the joints by pressing the butter-softened bread together.) Fill the mould with the stewed fruit and place the last round on top to seal.

Place in the preheated oven for 10 minutes and then reduce the heat to 190°C/375°F/gas mark 5 for 40 minutes and bake the charlotte until it is crisp and well-browned.

Chill for 3–4 hours in the fridge before taking out of the mould. Dust with caster sugar and serve with whipped cream.

POTATOES

*The swetest divarsion
that's under the sun
Is to sit by the fire
till the praties are done.* [1]

When we first moved to live in the country, our neighbours were just as shy of us as we were of them. Then strange things started to happen, and every fourth morning or so, we'd awake to find, as if by magic, sacks of potatoes left at the back door. Over the next few weeks the sacks continued to pile up, but gradually the mysterious case of the ever-appearing potatoes began to clear up, as the farmers started to make the deliveries in person, awkwardly pushing sacks before them as a means of introduction. Now we have an open invitation to come to the farmyards and raid the potato sheds whenever our own stocks show any sign of depletion. Indeed, we're so over-run by potatoes that we can feed not only ourselves but our entire extended families. I relate this somewhat sentimental tale because to us, as outsiders, those early unsourced deliveries were a warm and unassuming expression of welcome and acceptance into a rural farming community. However, the fact that potatoes were the vehicle for such communication is nothing strange in a country where no other food is capable of evoking so many mixed feelings of joy and misery.

Joy is the order of the day when the new year's potatoes go on sale in early summer. I always think that their arrival is Ireland's modest answer to the arrival of the new year's Beaujolais crop in France. New potatoes are the subject of feverish conversations between strangers on the streets, people phone the national radio stations lambasting the old crop and praising the new, and greengrocers chalk up gaudy window signs announcing to the world that the new stocks have arrived. Of course, the counterpoint to these exciting emotions of joy are those equally intense

70

memories of sorrow trawled up by reminiscences of the Great Famine in the mid-nineteenth century, when successive failures of the potato crop left the country socially and emotionally scarred until well into the twentieth century.

Legend suggests that Sir Walter Raleigh introduced the potato to Ireland in the late 1580s, there has also been speculation that potatoes were first washed onto Irish shores from the wrecks of the Spanish Armada in 1588, but whatever the mode of introduction, it had certainly arrived by the end of the sixteenth century. The late Austin Bourke, one of the most authoritative voices on the history of the potato in Ireland, has identified four general stages, outlining the gradual acceptance of the potato into the native diet through to the vegetable's eventual supremacy as a staple food by the late eighteenth century. He suggests that between 1590 and 1675 the potato was utilised as a supplementary food and as a stand-by against famine; and between 1675 and 1750 the potato was viewed as a valuable winter food by the poorer people, whose limited land resources could be used more productively, yielding far greater returns, when the potato replaced grain crops. From the mid-eighteenth century until 1810, a dangerous reliance on the vegetable amongst the poorer classes became evident, as the food became their staple for most of the year.

The development of new and more appetising potato varieties, notably the Black, the Irish Apple and the Cup, that remained edible over a longer time, encouraged this phenomenon. It was within this time frame that the English agronomist Arthur Young made his tour of Ireland, recording the entrenched position of the potato in the peasant diet. Of the peasantry of Magheraboy, County Sligo, he says:

> the food of the poor people is potatoes, milk, and herrings, with oaten bread in summer...They have an absolute bellyful of potatoes, and the children eat them as plentifully as they like. [2]

However, the bellyfuls that sustained the poor and labouring classes were, by the early nineteenth century, rapidly becoming a luxury of the past, as the period between 1810 and the Great Famine of 1845 became one of mounting distress, with localised famine and potato failures commonplace.

New inferior potato varieties were adopted on the promise of their excellent yields. In particular the lumper, described as 'a vile watery bulb, in which there is neither flavour nor nourishment', was increasingly cultivated despite its inherent disadvantages. One contemporary early nineteenth-century account sums up the plight of the poor and their forced reliance on the miserable lumper; a potato seen by many as fit only for cattle fodder:

> ... 'lumpers' have acquired an unwholesome quality after that day [Garland Sunday, the first Sunday in August]; those who can afford it cease to make these their sole food, and substitute oatmeal in some degree and use their deteriorated potatoes for feeding pigs. However, there are many cottiers who have no alternative but continuing to eat them or procuring others on credit at a high price. [3]

A swollen population, pressure on land resources, repressive rents and accelerating unemployment, caused in part by changing agricultural practices, left the rural poor in a state of utter destitution. So horrendous was the state of affairs that by 1833 the British government appointed a Commission of Inquiry under Richard Whatley, Archbishop of Dublin and a political economist, to ascertain the causes with a view to implementing relief. Alexis de Tocqueville, a French nobleman, who travelled to Ireland in 1835, pinpointed the origins of the misery. In conversation with Thomas Kelly, Secretary to the Board of Commissioners of National Education, he posed the question:

> According to what you tell me, although the agricultural population is poor, the land produces a great deal?

and the answer:

> The yields are immense. There is no country where the price of farms is higher. But none of this wealth remains in the hands of the people. The Irishman raises beautiful crops, carries his harvest

*to the nearest port, puts it on board an English vessel, and returns
home to subsist on potatoes. He rears cattle, sends them to
London, and never eats meat.* 4

The diet that Kelly refers to sustained the poor in good years and potatoes
were eaten in near incredible quantities. Witness after witness informed the
Poor Commission that 'the labouring man at all other times is accustomed
to live entirely on potatoes,' and anything from 3–5kg (about 7–12lb) of
potatoes was the normal repast per person per day. Naturally, therefore, in
such circumstances the potato crop commanded life and death:

*Life or death depends upon the potato crop; and when the year's
crop fails, starvation must ensue, for none of the former year's
crop can be preserved, and there is not enough of corn grown in
the country to feed the people after supplying the distilleries and
merchants, who must be supplied first, because they have plenty
of money.* 5

But all acknowledged that the worst time of the year was the period which
separated the old potatoes from the new. In general it was customary not
to pull the new crop until Lammas, the first day or first Sunday in August,
at the earliest. In particular the month of July, known variously as 'Hungry
July', 'The Bitter Six Weeks', or 'July of the cabbage' was a time of
temporary famine. Amhlaoibh Uí Shúileabháin records the end of this
period in his diary entry for the 31st of July (Lammas Eve) 1830:

*Here is an end to Famine Yellow-month, to July of the Famine.
Amen.* 6

Many however, through want, dug a portion of their crop long before
August, despite their small size. Some were obliged to take out the potatoes
when smaller than a pigeon's egg. Others stayed in bed until noon to avoid
the breakfast meal.

All of this was a prelude to the devastation that would follow the great
potato failures of 1845, '46 and '47, when a new agent, the presence of the

potato blight, *Phytophthora infestans*, wreaked an unprecedented level of hunger and fever. By 1851, at least one million of the Irish poor were dead. Another million had emigrated, many expiring on the infamous 'coffin ships' never reaching foreign shores. My great, great grand-uncle on my father's side was one of those who was forced to take passage on such ships and he, along with thousands of others, died without seeing America.

However, in good years before and after the Famine, a superabundance of potatoes gave a profusion of potato dishes. But more

often than not, the potatoes were simply boiled in their skins over the open fire until just bursting into a smile, and drained in shallow wicker woven baskets called *sciathóga*, which were then placed on the kitchen table or more usually in the middle of the floor in the run-down cabins of the poorer people. Once they were in place, the entire family, and perhaps the occasional hungry traveller, assembled in circular form around the heaped high baskets and collected onto themselves their own private caches of mealy soft potatoes. Noggins of fresh milk and pats of butter were handed around to mellow and sweeten the potato dinner. A sound piece of advice to diners on such occasions, as recalled in folk memory, was 'be eating one potato, peeling a second, have a third in your fist, and your eye on the fourth'. A common sight at such meal-time gatherings was the extra-long thumb nail cultivated on the right hand by each family member, for the purposes of potato peeling. When peeled in this fashion, the outer rind of the potato with its peculiar flavour, was not entirely lost.

In bad years, when yields were low or of poor quality, boiled potatoes were dressed 'with or without the bone or the moon'. The latter refers to boiled potatoes which were cooked sufficiently to the core so as to make them digestible by young children. However, when work was to be done or a long fast to be endured, 'praties with a bone or a moon' was the normal repast. Sir William Wilde, father of the celebrated Oscar writing in the mid-nineteenth century, explains these bizarre colloquialisms as follows:

Opposite: PRESERVED EGGS (see page 101)

74

*The heart of the potato was allowed, by checking the boiling at a
particular period, to remain parboiled, hard and waxy; when the
rest of the potato had been masticated in the usual manner, this
hard lump, about the size of a walnut, was bolted; and in this
manner nearly a stone of the root was taken into the stomach of
the Irish labourer per diem... it was grounded on a certain
knowledge of physiology. The stomach digested the well boiled
farinaceous portion of the potato within the space of a few hours,
and that having all been disposed of, the half-boiled lumps
remained behind, and a second digestion was commenced to
assimilate this portion of food, and convert it into nutritious, life-
sustaining material: which latter process lasted some hours longer,
and thus the cravings of hunger were warded off for five or six
hours after the original meal.* [7]

With a note of explanation in relation to *an ghealach* – the 'moon' – he adds,
'when a half-boiled potato is cut, the sections exhibit a central disk, with a
halo around it like the moon. English visitors have been puzzled by hearing
our servants reprimanded for "not boiling the moon out of the potato".

But if William Wilde's words seem too fanciful to be credible, then
there is no lack of contemporary evidence to substantiate his accounts.
Early nineteenth-century small farmers and labourers are often heard to
complain of meals with potatoes 'that were too soft to work upon'. And
Thomas Reid, who travelled through Ireland in the early 1820s, also refers
to the practice of half-boiling potatoes through necessity and hardship.
After a visit to a cabin in County Tyrone he records:

*The father was sitting on a stool and the mother on a kreel of turf;
one of the children had a straw box, the youngest even sprawling
on the floor, and five others were standing around the potato
basket. The potatoes were half-boiled. We always have our praties
hard, they stick to our ribs and we can fast longer that way.* [8]

Opposite: CHEESE,
CHIVE AND POTATO
PANCAKES (see page 101)

Despite or possibly because of such appalling
poverty, humour prevailed, giving rise to near

fantasy dishes such as 'potatoes and point'. This humorous appellation refers to the ritual of sitting around the *sciathóg* and, while the family munched through several pounds of boiled potatoes, all pointed longingly at the bacon flitches curing in the rafters, content in the knowledge that some day, maybe at Christmas or Easter, that very same piece of salty, smoky bacon would be added to the potato meal. Indeed, Sir William Wilde again has a slightly different version of the point dish and he maintains that anything used as a condiment, but more particularly the head of a salted herring, bruised into the bottom of a plate or small wooden cup, and sometimes called 'blind herring' was what constituted the dish. He also speaks of the following equally bizarre custom:

> *Occasionally, the salt herring itself was hung by a string*
> *from the chimney-brace, and each drop as it distilled therefrom*
> *was received upon the mealy mouthful by every individual*
> *in succession.* [9]

In the absence of meat or fish which, apart from on festive occasions, were beyond the means of the poorer classes, alternative condiments or 'kitchen' were devised to add a certain piquancy to the otherwise bland potato meal. Nettles, rape, dulse or occasionally some dried bream brought a welcome kick, as did the numerous potato dips, such as mustard dips, referred to by Arthur Young as early as the 1770s and of course, the favourite, onion dip; a simply made but much-loved concoction of onions, milk, flour and butter.

Apart from boiling, the cauldron and potato also came together to produce a variety of satisfying, starchy creamed potato dishes, recognised by a series of odd names like Champ, Colcannon and Pandy. Champ, a food savoured by the fairies, was really the mother of the other two and, like many potato dishes, its popularity and prevalence is evident in the host of colourful regional names applied to the dish. Names such as Poundies, Thump and Bruisy, strange as they may seem, all refer to the pounding or thumping process applied in their preparation. Once boiled, the crumbly balls of floury potatoes were pounded to a paste using a special wooden or iron pounder called a beetle. Very often in country homes, large 'pot-holes' could be seen, dug into the mud floor where the big iron pot was placed to steady it for the pounding or mashing process. This hard work was made easier by the liberal addition of fresh milk or cream and butter. The dish was then finished off with some sharp flavouring, usually scallions or young nettle tops, but leeks, onions, peas or chives were also welcome. Colcannon (see page 66) was simply a development of this dish, made by mixing cooked curly kale or cabbage into the creamy mess of potatoes. Both dishes were traditionally served in bowls, topped off with a good lump of melting butter and eaten by taking each spoonful from the outside and dipping it in the melted butter. Pandy is a dish of potatoes mashed with copious amounts of butter and flavoured with a sup of cream and salt. In theory it is child's fare but in reality everyone secretly harbours a love of the dish that evokes so many memories of childhood tastes and comforts.

The successful assimilation of the potato into the Irish diet is in part related to the fact that it could be successfully applied to the limited number of cooking utensils found hanging around the open fire in any Irish house. Like the relationship struck up between the potato and the cauldron referred to above, a similar one was forged between the potato and the griddle, giving us mouth-watering creations like Potato Cakes and Boxty. One theory is that Potato Cakes were conjured up in seasons when wheat or oatmeal was running scarce and to bulk out the cakes, quantities of mashed or raw grated potatoes (as with Boxty Bread) were added to stretch stocks and feed hungry bellies. The making of Boxty Bread brought an additional non-culinary bonus since the extracted liquid starch could be used to stiffen a father's shirt-collar or tighten the swing of a young girl's shift. The irrepressible William Wilde, with characteristic eloquence, sums it up as follows:

> It not only fed the great bulk of the peasantry, but it influenced their dress; it stiffened the brogue of the buckeen, and clear-starched the mob-cap of the collough. [10]

The other great merit of potatoes was that they could be roasted in the open air with the minimum of effort bringing maximum relish. Roast potatoes, or *bruthóga*, were usually enjoyed when a group or *meitheal* of workers came together to cut the turf, pick the potatoes, scutch the flax, mill the grain or supervise proceedings around the poteen stills. To make a break in the working day, a caste of potatoes was prepared by scooping out a hollow in a ditch and lighting a turf fire inside. Once the peat had died down, the coals were removed with wooden tongs and the unpeeled potatoes, wrapped in a skin of moist clay, were sat into the hot earth with a layer of half-burned turf placed on top. One worker, appointed cook, raked them out at the appropriate moment and the clay encrusted tubers were prepared by puncturing the skin to reveal a white, dry and mealy mass which was dressed with knobs of butter. Children were particularly partial to them, and there are accounts of babies not more than three months old munching their way, with toothless gums, through these soft treats. Roast potatoes mashed with cream were believed to be effective in the treatment of cuts and wounds, while rubbing one onto warts and then abandoning it on some roadway ensured the demise of the ugly skin blemish.

POTATO CAKES

> *Did you ever take potato cakes or boxty to the school?*
> *Tucked underneath your oxter, with your book, and slide and rule,*
> *and when teacher wasn't looking, a big bite you did take.*
> *Of the creamy, mealy, sweet potato cake.* [11]

This is just one verse of a popular song devoted entirely to the pleasures of eating potato dishes like Boxty and Colcannon. Boxty and Potato Cakes, unlike Colcannon, were portable and could be carried as a snack to ward off hunger. Potato Cakes are also known in Ireland as 'tatties' or 'parleys'.

Serves 4

450G (1LB) POTATOES (GOLDEN WONDERS OR KERR'S PINKS ARE GOOD)
1 TEASPOON SALT AND A PINCH OF FRESHLY GROUND BLACK PEPPER
25–55G (1–2OZ) BUTTER
110G (4OZ) PLAIN FLOUR
A LITTLE BUTTER OR BACON FAT (IF FRYING)

Wash and scrub the potatoes, but don't peel, and boil in slightly salted boiling water (making sure that there is enough water to cover the potatoes) until they are tender. Once cool enough to handle, drain and peel potatoes. It's important to use potatoes that are still hot as these make the best potato cakes.

Mash the potatoes to a smooth consistency, ensuring that there are no lumps. Season with salt and freshly ground pepper and pour in the melted butter. Add and knead in enough flour to make a pliable and easily manageable dough. (Don't overdo the kneading or the finished cakes will be tough and heavy.)

Roll out onto a lightly floured board to form a round of about 0.5–1cm (¼–½in) thickness. Cut the round into triangles or farls, or make small individual round cakes. Cook on a hot dry griddle until both sides are mottled and golden brown. The cakes can also be fried on a hot pan in some melted butter or bacon fat.

Serve hot, spread with butter and honey or sugar and a sprinkling of ground ginger or split them with a little butter and eat them with smoked bacon and fried juicy mushroom caps for breakfast.

POTATO PUDDINGS

After potato breads and creamed potato dishes, potato puddings enjoyed universal appeal in Ireland. Indeed their popularity is evident in the myriad of different regional pudding recipes. Sometimes they were savoury, other times sweet, enlivened with sugar, saffron, butter and eggs or spiced with the addition of caraway seeds and mixed spices. The northern counties, traditionally the strong orchard growing areas, boast a Potato Apple Pudding, which must surely be first cousin to that other northern speciality, Potato Apple Cake.

Potato puddings do not, as might be expected, require an oven to ensure their successful preparation. The bastible pot or 'pot oven' did just as well, which meant, of course, that potato puddings could be prepared in most rural homes despite the absence of a conventional oven. Packed into the bastible, the pudding was set on the crane hanging over the open fire, and when the lid was covered in a blanket of turf the resultant puddings held their own unique flavour. Potato puddings were always made up for the Hallowe'en night feast, often hiding a ring; a portent of an early marriage for the lucky one who found it.

My favourite pudding recipe comes from the pen of Florence Irwin, who in turn acquired it from one of her many correspondents. I like it because it's a highly active recipe, as is clear in the great number of action verbs; 'knead, press, fill, make holes', and so on. After such hard physical toil, what better way to recover than with soothing potato pudding?

> *Take about 2lb smoothly mashed potatoes. Knead on a board with flour as when making potato-cake. Add salt, pepper, and allspice to taste. Make into a ball. Have a warm, well-greased pot-oven ready. Press the potato mixture into the pot. Make four holes with the pot-stick. Fill these with fresh milk. Cover the pot. Place over peat coals, with the same on the lid. Bake for 4 hours.* [12]

BABY POTATO PIES

This is my pastry-encrusted minor version of the larger potato pies.

Makes 14–16 pies in a conventional bun tin or 12 in a muffin tin

Shortcrust pastry:

225G (8OZ) PLAIN FLOUR

I TEASPOON SALT

150G (5OZ) BUTTER, CUBED

I EGG YOLK

2 TABLESPOONS WATER

Filling:

5–6 LARGE POTATOES

110G (4OZ) BUTTER

A LITTLE HOT MILK

1 LARGE ONION, FINELY CHOPPED

LARGE BUNCH MIXED FRESH HERBS, FINELY CHOPPED (THYME IS A MUST,
  PARSLEY, CHIVES, 2–3 SAGE LEAVES)

SALT AND FRESHLY GROUND BLACK PEPPER TO TASTE

1 EGG, BEATEN

Preheat the oven to 220°C/425°F/gas mark 7.

Sift the flour and salt into a bowl. Add the butter. Rub the butter
into the flour with your hands until it resembles fine, crumbly
breadcrumbs. Make sure you constantly lift and aerate the
mixture. Make a well in the centre of the bowl and add the egg
yolk and water. In a circular fashion, gradually draw the mixture
into the wet ingredients and work together to form a soft but
pliable dough. Turn onto a floured surface and knead lightly to
smoothen the consistency of the dough. Work into a ball, wrap in
cling film and leave to rest and chill in the refrigerator for at least
30 minutes before use.

Wash the potatoes and boil them in their skins until soft but
not too tender. Drain, then return them to the pan. Cover with a
clean towel and leave them to finish cooking in their own steam.
Replace the pan lid and leave for several minutes. Peel and cut the
potatoes into quarters, return to the pan and mash with the butter
and enough hot milk to made a smooth, lump-free mixture. Stir in
the chopped onion and finely chopped herbs. Season to taste.

On a cool, floured surface, roll out the chilled pastry into a
thin circle. With a small pastry cutter (10cm/4in-diameter) cut out
enough pastry cases. Line the tin. Spoon in a generous portion of
potato filling. Cut pastry lids from the remaining pastry. These
must be substantially smaller than the pastry cases. Place the lids
in position, sealing each with the lower pastry case with your
index finger. With a skewer or knitting kneedle, make a steam hole
in the centre of each pie. Brush each with a little beaten egg and
bake in the preheated oven for 25–30 minutes or until the pies are
crisp and golden brown. Remove from the oven but leave to rest in
the tin for some minutes before easing out.

WILLIAM WILDE'S POTATO FRITTERS

William Wilde offers this unusual and rich recipe for potato fritters. They can be augmented by combining the potato slices with wafer-thin slices of apple or fresh peaches, before they're dipped in the batter.

> *A very delicious dish may be made by slicing raw potatoes to the thickness of a crown piece, allowing them to dry for some time, and then steeping them in brandy for two or three hours, until they absorb a sufficiency of that fluid. Dip each slice in a rich batter, then fry them to a light brown, and dust them, before serving, with powdered sugar and grated lemon peel.* [13]

STAMPY

Stampy is a deluxe version of Boxty Bread, made with cream, sweetened with sugar and spiced with caraway seeds (see photograph opposite page 50). It was served on special occasions, like the end of the potato harvest, or specially prepared to celebrate any of the secular and religious festivals that punctuate the Irish year. It was a particularly favourite dish on Hallowe'en night. The combination of flavours was much admired by children who joined in the preparation by making graters from old tin cans, punched with an awl, so as to pare their lumper potatoes down for the Stampy feast.

Serves 4–8

225G (8OZ) RAW POTATOES

225G (8OZ) COOKED POTATO, MASHED

25G (1OZ) BUTTER

55ML (2FL OZ) DOUBLE CREAM

2 TEASPOONS CARAWAY SEEDS

110G (4OZ) CASTER SUGAR

225G (8OZ) SELF RAISING FLOUR

Preheat the oven to 200°C/400°F/gas mark 6, leaving a floured baking sheet in the oven to heat.

Peel and grate the raw potatoes then transfer them to the centre of a clean tea-towel and, whilst holding the cloth over a bowl, wring tightly to extract the starchy liquid. Leave this to settle until the starch separates and rests at the bottom of the bowl. This process will take at least 2 hours. Transfer the grated potatoes to another bowl. Meanwhile, mash the cooked potatoes with the butter and cream. While waiting for the starch to settle, sit the mashed potatoes on top of the grated ones in the bowl to prevent them from browning. When the starch has settled, pour off and discard the surface liquid and add the remaining starch to the mashed and grated potatoes, mixing well. Season with salt and freshly ground pepper.

Mix the caraway seeds through the sugar and add to the potatoes. Sift the flour and mix this in too to make a soft pliable dough. Turn the dough onto a floured surface and knead lightly. Place on the heated baking sheet and cut into 4–8 farls. Bake for 35–40 minutes. Serve hot with butter.

CEREALS

Wheatlet, son of Milklet,
Honeyed Butter-roll. [1]

Soda bread, soda scones, sweet buttery country cakes, oatcakes, bran loaves, apple tarts, potato cakes, potato apple cakes, maize bread, buttermilk bread, crusty wheaten loaves, gingerbread, caraway cakes, plum cakes, tea bracks, barm bracks, simnel cakes, and pancakes – truly, no matter how hard you try, you can't but fall victim to Ireland's impressive baking tradition. More so than any other aspect of food and cooking, the Irish exude a pride in their bread- and cake-making talents; talents that until well into the early twentieth century were nurtured and perfected using the simplest of equipment, the metal cake griddle and the cast iron pot oven (commonly known as the 'bastible pot'). From earliest times, baking was part of the Irish psyche, so much so that the seventh-to eighth-century law-text *Cáin Íarraith* (Law of the Fosterage Fee), which outlines the rules of fosterage, stipulates that foster parents are legally obliged to teach the skills of flour-sieving, kneading and baking to young girls. Furthermore, the same early legal texts also look upon baking utensils as indispensable kitchen items, and anyone who damages or misappropriates the griddle, the griddle slice, the kneading trough, the sieve or the wooden measuring vessels is subject to legal procedure. In the absence of a built-up oven, most Irish farmhouse breads were of a flat variety and oatcakes, barley bannocks, wheaten loaves and maslin breads were served with a variety of relishes. Bacon, with at least an inch of fat, was certainly the most popular condiment, but on non-meat days garlic, onions, leeks, curds, cheese, apples, sea vegetables, buttermilk and herrings filled the hungry gap.

When the Anglo-Normans, with their spicy cuisine, settled in Ireland in the twelfth and thirteenth centuries, they brought with them the concept of oven-fired wheaten leavened breads, and in time bake houses became part and parcel of Irish city life. In the same fashion, the Elizabethans and Jacobites introduced rich and gooey plum pottages and spiced fruit loaves. Fynes Moryson, Secretary to the Lord Deputy, Lord Mountjoy, noted the availability of English-style breads in the Irish cities of the early seventeenth century:

> *In cities they have such bread as ours, but of a sharp savor, and some mingled with anise-seeds and baked like cakes, and that only in the houses of the better sort.* [2]

And in gentrified circles the range of fancy baked goods would take a tear from the most sophisticated eye. When Miss Sandford called on Carton House in County Kildare in the eighteenth century, she was presented with the following baffling array:

> *We have an immense table, chocolate, honey, hot bread, cold bread, brown bread, white bread, green bread, and all coloured breads and cakes.* [3]

The nineteenth century was the real watershed in Irish bread-making. The introduction of baking soda in the early 1800s gave those without access to kitchen ovens the opportunity to produce home-made raised breads simply and quickly. The hearth, the bastible and the skilful turn of the woman's hand combined to create a knockout fine quality Irish soda bread, whose curls of hot steam wafted from Irish rural kitchens on a daily basis. Around this time, maize also made its first appearance in Ireland, and maize breads and dumplings joined an ever-increasing repertoire of Irish home-baked goods. Sadly, however, the status of home-baked breads came under attack in the late nineteenth century with the widespread availability of professionally produced 'white baker's bread', which was seen by many as superior to anything the woman of the house could turn out. In a bizarre turn of events, shop-bought breads came to dominate and usurp the older bread staples. Visitors to Irish homes were now welcomed with refined wheat loaves rather than with piping hot oatcakes and freshly baked sodas.

But apart from breads, the fruits of the cereal harvest were also directed to the production of porridges and gruels. Indeed, oats were probably consumed much more in the form of porridge than as bread, since porridge is easily prepared and highly digestible relative to coarser oaten cakes. That porridge and stirabout were synonymous with the Irish is clear from Jerome's comment on the heresiarch Celestius whom he describes as *paltibus Scottus praegraratus*, 'a great fool of a fellow, swelled out with Irish stirabout'. [4]

Since medieval times, porridge and gruel were valued for their nutritional and sustaining properties, and were regularly recommended for the young, the sick and those ailing. As early as the tenth century, Ireland's seriously no-nonsense community of penitential monks recognised the positive values of porridge and called for its inclusion in the diet of menstruating nuns!

> *During the monthly sickness of the daughters of the Church, they are excused from vigils, morning and evening, so long as it lasts, and gruel is to be made for them at tierce, [the third of the seven canonical hours – about 9am] at whatever time this happens, because it is right that this sickness should have attention.* [5]

Such kindness, however, didn't extend to the nuns' male counterparts, who were stuck with watery gruels as their penitential fare, and one king-pin in monastic circles, Màel Ruain, of the Tallaght Monastery, fearful of its potential for exciting the libido of Ireland's male penitents, proclaimed the proper eating procedure for watery gruels:

> *… but I shall counsel him to drink by sips; for this quenches thirst and a man finds less sensual pleasure and satisfaction in sips than in draught, when he is thirsty.* [6]

OATCAKES

Oats are ideally suited to Ireland's damp climate and they thrive in the country's rich, dark, acidic soils; by consequence the crop's high yields made oatcakes an ever-present feature of the diet. John Dunton, the English traveller and bookseller, came across oatcakes in the homes of both the peasant and wealthy alike. In a poor cabin of the late 1690s in Iar-Connaught, he was offered 'oaten cakes, along with a greate roll of fresh butter of three pound at least'. In the days following in the house of the wealthier O'Flaghertie he received beef and mutton and '...at the upper end where the lady sate was placed on a heap of oaten cakes above a foot high.' [7]. On occasions of communal eating, around for example the harvest or threshing, oatcakes the size of a cartwheel (called in Irish *Multachán*) were baked on an enormous griddle for the hungry men of the fields.

Traditionally oats was ground to a meal in a hand-mill or rotary quern and mixed with a little butter and hot water to a stiff paste. The thinly rolled dough was then placed on a hot griddle or heated flagstone, divided into farls or 'pointers' and left to bake. After sufficient baking, the cake was dried out, resting against a hardening stand, before the open fire. Dunton again sets the scene,

> *...when she had ground her oates upon the querns or hand mill-stones, with a little water she made a triangular cake which she reared up before the fire against a little wodden stool made like a tripod...* [8]

If oatcakes are properly made, they will last for several weeks, even months. Their lasting qualities therefore, made them a good travelling food and many emigrants to America set off with bags of oatcakes to sustain them on their journey.

Serves 4–8

225G (8OZ) FINELY GROUND OATMEAL

1 TEASPOON SALT

25G (1OZ) BUTTER

150ML–180ML (5–6FL OZ) HOT WATER

Preheat the oven to 160°C/325°F/gas mark 3, leaving a baking tray in the oven to heat.

Mix the oatmeal and salt in a bowl. Then rub in the butter with your fingers. For a more even absorption of the fat, melt the butter and pour over the oatmeal. Mix well. Add enough water to make a stiff, though slightly sticky, paste. Transfer the dough to a floured baking sheet or a lightly buttered griddle or flat pan.

With heavily floured hands, push the paste from the centre outwards, working predominantly with the centre of the palms and the fingers. Shape into a circle about 0.5cm (¼in) thick. Lightly score the surface into 4–8 farls or triangles. Transfer to the heated baking tray and bake in the cool oven for 35–40 minutes or, if using a pan, allow to cook over the lowest heat for about 1 hour, turning for the last 5 minutes to firm the other surface.

Serve hot with plenty of butter. For a light meal, serve with grilled bacon and whole fried, juicy field mushrooms.

IRISH MUESLI

The story of modern-day muesli supposedly begins in Switzerland in the late nineteenth century, when the nutritionist Bircher-Benner devised a cereal mixture with health promoting properties. He advised a mixture based on raw cereals with added fruit and nuts, which over time became a popular breakfast dish. However, I think that a rudimentary form of Bircher-Benner's creation was current in Ireland as early as the ninth century. Around this time, a community of penitential monks, known as the *Céli Dé* (the people of God) suffered through life on a less than exciting dish called *brothchán*. At its worst, this was a miserable watery gruel taken routinely on weekdays. However, the intrigue begins with the rules concerning the monks' Sunday fare. According to one piece of Penitential literature, *brothchán* is to be made on Sundays with 'good milk', served with additional relishes and eaten before midday office. The relishes mentioned are 'a spoonful of honey' and 'all sorts of fruit of all seasons', which in medieval Ireland meant apples, both wild and cultivated, blackberries, sloes, wild raspberries and strawberries, and hazelnuts; all of which suggest that the dish in this instance could well have been an early version of muesli.

88

Another curious Irish dish prevalent as late as the nineteenth century was *práipín*, closely akin to muesli but taken without the fruit and nuts. One woman from around the Clonmel area of County Tipperary described it as:

> *whole wheat grains which are dried in a pan over the open fire and are then ground into a kind of meal in a quern. It is then taken just like a breakfast food with milk and perhaps sugar.* [9]

So, I rest my case; the Irish invented muesli!

Allow 50–75g (2–3oz) flake oatmeal per serving

Mix with grated apple, halved hazelnuts, blackberries and raspberries.
Pour on fresh milk and top with honey and natural yoghurt.

YELLOWMEAL BREAD

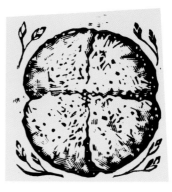

Barnaby Blacker came to Ireland in the late 1980s to train at the Ballymaloe Cookery School in East Cork. Before long, his obvious gift for concocting all things sweet enabled him to start up his own restaurant and confectionery shop in Cork. One of the house specials is yellowmeal bread, a wonderfully soft maize soda bread. Now, apart from his flair in the kitchen, there's nothing too odd about the Barnaby tale, but that was until the day he revealed himself to be the great, great, great grandson of Sir Robert Peel of Drayton Manor in Staffordshire. Peel was the British Prime Minister in 1845, the year which saw the beginning of the Great Irish Famine. In the autumn of 1845, following the disastrous potato harvest, Peel, on behalf of the Government, ordered the purchase of £100,000 worth of maize to relieve the impending food crisis. In March 1846, maize meal went on sale at a penny a pound, for those with the strength and money to procure it. But in 1846, yellowmeal was no stranger to Ireland. It had made its first appearance in the country in the early decades of the nineteenth century, when it was introduced by the British Government to offset the problems of recurrent potato failures and poor cereal harvests. In this pre-Famine period, the distribution of inferior quality maize, which was unfit for human consumption, caused widespread illness and soon the corn became a loathsome foodstuff. Despised and rejected by many, it earned the nickname 'Peel's Brimstone', an appellation which recognised its deep yellow colour and the man who imported it.

But the sale of £100,000 worth of maize in March 1846 was in response to an entirely new and dire development, hitherto unknown to the Irish peasant farmer. The first outbreak of potato blight in 1845 destroyed much of the potato crop, and food shortages were severe and worsening by the late spring of 1846. So famished were the masses that now they rioted, not in rejection of the foodstuff, but rushing in order to gather up as much as they could. Cork was one of the first centres to sell the corn and by the summer of 1846, was selling 600 tons per week.

Nonetheless, ignorance of the proper preparation techniques was still rampant. This was made worse by the fact that much of the corn was badly ground and was sold in coarse and lumpy form. In many a hovel cauldrons of boiling maize spat ferociously, and young children were whipped from around the hearth in the belief the hissing mass would erupt and scald them. Others mistakenly believed that the cauldron of maize should be left to boil throughout the night. In truth, the lumpy maize needed lengthy boiling, and one folk belief associated with it maintained that the devil's mother had her hand in it, thus preventing it cooking.

Despite these initial culinary setbacks, by the late nineteenth century maize was a feature of the Irish diet, consumed in the form of maize porridge, bread and dumplings. The account below, given by a woman born in 1867, sums up the pattern of culinary uncertainty followed by gradual acceptance of a new and strange foodstuff:

> *My father and mother went through the famine. My father got for his week's wages making roads, One st. or One ½st. of Indian Meal – That was after the famine. The women did not know how*

to cook the Indian meal. When boiling, it splattered all round. They did not know when it was cooked. Some people saying, the meal should be left cooking all night. Some going as far as saying the Devil's mother had a hand in it, thus preventing the Indian meal from getting cooked. So the women got instructions how to cook it, but as many had neither oven or pan on which to bake the cake they baked it on a green leaf of cabbage covered by another leaf of cabbage on the hearth.

The women did not know how to use the flour. When making a cake they frequently put a cup of soda to a saucepan of flour, or sometimes half and half. It took the women some time to learn how to make Soda Bread. [10]

By a strange and ironic twist of fate, yellowmeal bread is back on the streets of Cork, all thanks to Barnaby Blacker.

Makes 1 loaf
175G (6OZ) FINE MAIZE FLOUR
275G (10OZ) PLAIN WHITE FLOUR
1 LEVEL TEASPOON SALT
1 LEVEL TEASPOON BICARBONATE OF SODA (BREAD SODA)
340ML (12FL OZ) BUTTERMILK OR SOUR MILK
Preheat the oven to 230°C/450°F/gas mark 8, leaving a baking tray in the oven to heat.

Sieve all the dry ingredients into a large mixing bowl. Give them a quick mix with your hand before making a well in the centre. Pour in nearly all the milk. Steadying the bowl with one hand, use the other to draw in all the flour to make a soft and very pliable dough. Add the rest of the milk if you need it.

Turn the dough onto a floured board and shape it into a round of about 2.5cm (1½in) thickness. Firmly cut a cross into the surface of the dough, transfer to the hot baking tray and bake for 35–40 minutes in the oven. Test with a skewer to ensure thorough baking.

When tapped on the bottom the loaf should make a hollow sound. Eat hot with melting butter. It is equally good served cold with chutney and cold home cooked ham.

SODA BREAD

Soda bread must be the most renowned and savoured of all Irish traditional breads, however, in contrast to items like oatcakes or wheaten loaves, it is a relative newcomer to the Irish culinary scene. The leavening agent, bicarbonate of soda, was first introduced into Ireland in the first half of the nineteenth century and, by the second half of the century, soda bread had become popular throughout the country. Its popularity may in part be attributed to the fact that when soda is combined with sour milk, or buttermilk, it produces a very light and palatable leavened wheat bread that can easily be produced at home. This bread is very quick to prepare, in contrast to the more time-consuming task of preparing traditional coarse oaten breads. It is also ideally suited to a limited range of baking utensils; the pot oven, or bastible, and the flat iron griddle. In comparison to the other leavening agents of yeast, barm, sourdough and eggs, that soda provided a convenient, storable and predictable leaven that quickly became the standard.

Traditionally, a cross was cut into the bread, which helped the bread to bake evenly and assisted the cutting of the round loaf afterwards. The custom was especially emphasised on Good Friday in honour of the crucifixion, but household superstition holds that the practice is 'to let the devil out'.

Soda bread is one of the easiest of breads to prepare and the secret to its success lies in a very light kneading of the dough.

450G (1LB) PLAIN FLOUR

1 TEASPOON SALT

1 TEASPOON BICARBONATE OF SODA (BREAD SODA)

340–370ML (12–13FL OZ) BUTTERMILK

Preheat the oven to 230°C/450°F/gas mark 8, and leave a floured baking tray in the oven to heat.

Sieve all the dry ingredients into a bowl and mix well. Make a well in the centre and pour in most of the buttermilk. Working round the bowl, draw the flour into the buttermilk with your hand, working in a circular fashion until all the milk has been absorbed. When the dough comes together it should feel sticky and pliable. If you feel the dough needs it, add the rest of the milk. Turn onto a floured working surface and, kneading lightly, give it just a couple of turns to fix into a round shape. Using the palm of your hand, flatten into a round of about 5cm/2in thickness and cut a deep cross into the surface of the dough. Transfer to the heated baking tray and bake in a very hot oven for 15 minutes then reduce the heat to 200°C/400°F/gas mark 6 and bake for another 20–30 minutes.

Test the loaf with a skewer, alternatively tap the bottom of the loaf. If it is baked properly it will make a hollow sound.

Serve hot with butter and fruity jam.

EGGS & DAIRY PRODUCE

The fort we reached was beautiful,
with works of custards thick,
smooth pillars of old cheese,
fine beams of mellow cream. [1]

In Irish the word for a cow is *bó*; the word for road is *bóthar*, originally a term describing a cow track; and the word for a boy is *buachaill*, literally a cow-boy, a term which recalls an era when the herding and caring of cattle fell to the young boys in the community. I relay this simple Irish lesson because I think that these three words, fundamental to the vocabulary of any language, sum up succinctly the prevalence and significance of cattle, particularly milch cows and their dairy produce, in the diet of the Irish until well into the seventeenth century. Until this period, the native Gaelic diet was dominated by dairy produce for at least one half of the year. From roughly May until late autumn the great milk herds of Kerry, Shorthorn and Moiled cows, filled the cauldrons and bellies of the Irish with esteemed white meats or *bàn bídh*. At a time when meat was a luxury and a rare treat, whitemeats were welcomed as a valuable source of protein, calcium and most importantly fat, a layer of which helped many a Jack Sprat to make it through the lean and hungry months of winter and spring. But of course the other merit of dairy produce was that it was easily converted into storable cheeses and heavily salted butter, which was and still is the most savoured and versatile of all traditional Irish foods.

Between the two Celtic festivals of *Beltene* (1st of May) and *Samhain* (1st of November) the lush upland pastures were grazed by milk cows which in turn supplied milk in abundance for use in the preparation of sour milk drinks, curds, soft and hard cheeses and of course fresh and salted butter. During this summer period of temporary transhumance or 'booleying', as it was known in Ireland, the tending of the herds, often a mixture of cattle and goats, fell to the young boys and girls who erected temporary dwellings in the upland slopes. Here, living a near independent existence, away from the scorn of the adult world, the youngsters worked and played, sending the prepared dairy products back down the mountain slopes. There is some supporting evidence to suggest that the practice of booleying continued through to the modern period. Even as late as the early twentieth century the story-teller Tadhg Ó Buachalla, better known as 'The Tailor', from Gougane Barra, County Cork, could recall a time when going to the 'booley' was commonplace:

> About the end of May, or early in June, when the potatoes had all been used up, and the next year's potatoes set, those who had hill-land, extending from what was arable, would take the cows up there. They might also have a couple of goats or more. Beside a rock, up in the hill, a little house would have been built, roofed with scraws [strips of sods]. There they would make butter. Also they would boil goats' milk and crack it so as to make curds and whey. [2]

Milk, curds and soft cheeses bulked out the summer time diet, and their prevalence is evident in the fact that they were demanded as taxes by the local aristocracy. The seventh-to eighth-century law text, *Cáin Aicillne ('Law of Base Clientship')* for example, demanded that farmers yield an annual return of a 'cauldron full of new milk, to be boiled to sweet cheese curds with butter'. In general, tubs of curds flavoured with wild garlic, wood sorrel and salted butter or sweetened with honey and hazelnuts were widespread summer sustenance, while at the same time, milk and buttermilk quenched the summertime thirst. Interestingly, however, it seems that *lemnacht* or fresh milk did not enjoy popularity as a beverage and it was more usual to take milk in a soured state. Milk in a variety of souring states is mentioned in the eleventh-century *Aisling meic Conglinne (The Vision of Mac Conglinne)*. Aniér, the main character of this epic poem samples a drink:

of very thick milk, of milk not too thick, of milk of long thickness, of milk of medium thickness, of yellow bubbling milk, the swallowing of which needs chewing, of the milk that makes a snorry bleat of a ram as it rushes down the gorge. [3]

As late as 1690, an English seventeenth-century writer, John Stevens noted:

the people generally being the greatest lovers of milk, I ever saw, which they eat and drink about twenty several sorts of ways and what is strangest, love it best when sourest. [4]

Thick soured milk, known as *bainne clabair* (thick milk), was anglicised to 'bonnyclabber' by a host of sixteenth- and seventeenth-century travellers to Ireland, many of whom note its prevalence in the diet. Once again Fynes Moryson's keen eye notes its presence and indeed the wider status of milk herds in Irish society:

They feed most on white meats, and esteem for a great dainty sour curds, vulgarly called by them 'bonaclabbe'. And for this cause they watchfully keep their cows and fight for them as for their religion and life; and when they are almost starved, yet they will not kill a cow, except it be old and yield no milk. [5]

Incidentally, milking was considered exclusively women's work and this is illustrated in one incident from the *Life of St Brigid*. The saint encounters a downcast man and on enquiring as to the cause of his gloom, he replies:

my whole household is ill and there is no woman to milk the cows. [6]

The implication is that the man is socially exempt from the task and accordingly Brigid orders her maidens to milk the cows for him. But until well into the twentieth century, the division of labour on rural farms saw women, and women only, involved in milking and poultry-keeping. As late as the mid-twentieth century, two American anthropologists encountered

this rigid adherence to specific gender roles:

> *for a man to concern himself with a woman's work, such as the*
> *sale of eggs or the making of butter, is the subject of derisive*
> *laughter, while a woman's smaller hands make it 'natural' for her*
> *to be a better hand at milking cows.* 7

But the milking women of Ireland were not only hard-working but also highly innovative; should the milk cow not render milk in the absence of her calf, the women employed the effective technique of 'tail-blowing'. This strange practice was recorded by Fynes Moryson in his *Itinerary* (1617).

> *Yea when these cowes thus madly denie their milke, the women*
> *wash their hands in cowes dung, and so gently stroke their dugges,*
> *yea, put their hands into the cowes taile, and with their mouthes*
> *blow into their tailes, that with this manner (as it were)*
> *enchantment, they may draw milk from them.* 8

The indigenous cheese-making tradition is everywhere apparent in the early medieval sources where soft and hard cheeses are regularly mentioned. The diversity of shape and texture of both the pressed and unpressed cheeses was enthusiastically interwoven into the imagery of many of the medieval tales. Thus for example, the ninth-century tale *Togail Bruidne Da Derga (The Destruction of Da Derga's Hostel)* mentions the fierce warrior, Iugcél Cáech who boasted that:

> *the size of a soft large cheese [Maethal] was each of his buttocks.* 9

Likewise the soft, unpressed sweet curd cheese *millsén* is referred to in the eleventh-century tale, *Aisling meic Conglinne (The Vision of Mac Conglinne):*

> *Every oar we plied in New-milk Lake would send its sea-sand of*
> *cheese curds to the surface.* 10

as is the hard swollen cheese *tanach*:

> *a bristling rubble dyke of stone, of swollen hard cheeses.* [11]

Once prepared, the cheeses were left to ripen and mature in the underground passages or souterraines attached to many of the raths or earthen ringforts, and in line with milking and butter-making, cheese-making was also considered women's work. However, in the early medieval period at least, the woman's contribution to the effective running of the dairy economy was recognised and rewarded. So much so that if the woman decided to divorce her husband, if for example he engaged in offensive behaviour like broadcasting the secrets of the marital bed, then she was entitled to walk away from the marriage with appropriate compensation and most of the cheeses in store.

Sadly, the seventeenth century was to see the decline of the native cheese-making tradition. Successive decades of political and land upheavals wreaked havoc with the native economy. Moreover, the passing of the Cattle Acts by the London Parliament further compounded the ailing dairy economy. The first Act, passed in 1663, imposed hefty tariffs on the exportation of cattle from Ireland, while the Act of 1666 introduced an all-out embargo of the exportation of cattle, sheep, pigs, beef, pork and bacon from Ireland to Britain. Such measures led directly to the development of the provision trade, which saw Ireland exporting its farm produce in the form of salted beef and salted butter. By the eighteenth century, the fattening of calves destined for the export beef market and the growing butter-making industry absorbed the country's milk and cream stocks, thus marking the end of the white-meat or *bánbídh* (milk, curds and cheeses) tradition which had for so long characterised native Irish food patterns. However, a limited number of farmers, in particular those with herds large enough to give a surplus of milk and cream after butter-making, continued to produce cheeses, though on a much reduced scale and mostly for domestic use. A glance at many eighteenth- and nineteenth-century 'Big House' inventories listing cheese-making equipment would seem to indicate that cheese-making continued to enjoy favour, at least within the upper echelons of Irish society.

Likewise, contemporary 'receipt' books frequently include instructions for sweet curds and soft-cheeses. However, in recent years the emergence of a plethora of a small artisan cheese-makers, crafting a wide variety of cows', goats' and sheeps' cheeses has taken Ireland and, indeed, Europe by storm.

But of all the dairy products, butter is the one that has endured as the Irish favourite; despite all the bad press. It holds pride of place at all meals, it brings a certain character and an unmistakable taste to all baked goods, and is even incorporated into the process of poteen distillation in the belief that it will bring a smoothness to the finished treasured liquor. Traditionally, butter's strong position in the Irish diet was, in part, due to its relationship with that other Irish staple, the oatcake. The well-known folklorist, Estyn Evans, maintained that the staple in Ireland was butter and oatcake, rather than oatcake and butter, since the harsh and abrasive nature of oatcakes demanded copious quantities of butter to assist the swallowing process. But butter did not remain loyal to its first love, and when the potato was introduced to Ireland, both struck up an inseparable relationship. Indeed, the everlasting popularity of butter may be attributed to the fact that it complements a host of different foods. Butter, then, has withstood the test of time because of its skill in striking up a flirtatious relationship with anything from potatoes to currany cake to undressed vegetables and steamy hot soda cakes.

In many rural farmsteads, butter was churned once or twice a week to meet the family's needs; though not in the sensational manner described at the end of the seventeenth century by the English bookseller and traveller, John Dunton. He recorded his observations of his Irish tour in a series of letters in 1698; in a cabin in Iar-Connaught, Connemara, he was unwillingly subject to the following churning performance!

for my landlady, after she had acquitted herselfe of the cake, fell to washing her hands and arms, and immediately brings to the hearth a small wodden churn, narrow at the mouth and bottle-bellied.

99

She seates her in the same posture as when at the querns, with the
churn between her leggs, and claps in her right arm almost up to
the arm pitt, which she made use of it instead of a churn staff, and
as the milke flasht out of the vessell upon her thighs she stroakt it
of with her left into it againe; the butter was not long comeing,
nor do I wonder that Irish butter should smel rank and strong if
all be made after this manner, for surely the heate which this
labour put the good wife in must unavoidabley have made some of
the essence of arms pitts tricle down her arm into the churn... [12]

TURFY EGGS

Denis Hyland, a well known photographer from Cork, told me of how he cooked eggs as a boy when cutting turf or peat in the bogs of County Kerry. Working parties usually set off for the bog in the early morning, and as turf-cutting was a day-long affair, each man was obliged to carry nourishing fare to sustain the back-breaking work. Soda bread parcelled up in brown paper with a few ducks' eggs was popular bog-fare, but while the soda-bread was baked fresh by the woman of the house before the men set off, it was always the custom to leave the cooking of the eggs as near as possible to the time they were to be consumed. When much of the turf had been cut and spread to dry, a welcome shout would go up announcing a well-deserved break in work for rest and refreshment. It was at this point that the old tin canisters were pulled out, filled with bog-water and when the ducks' eggs were slipped in, all was set over a

turf fire to boil. After boiling each man carefully beheaded his egg, and then dexterously placed a little wisp of burning turf onto the soft yolk. This process served to singe and seal the egg, while at the same time imbued it with a peculiar turfy taste. Then, once the spoon had broken through the egg crust, all was gobbled down with mouthfuls of soda bread. Denis declares that it's a taste he'll never forget.

TO PRESERVE EGGS

Cork City is home to a number of unique Irish traditional foods, not least among them the famous and wonderfully rich buttered eggs (see photograph opposite page 74). Just three ingredients are required for their successful preparation; freshly laid hot eggs, fresh unsalted butter and a speedy dexterous pair of hands. As soon as the hen lays, the egg must be whipped away and rolled between the palms of the hands that have been smeared with fresh butter. The hot egg soaks in the butter and, once cooled, this forms an airtight seal, keeping the egg fresh well into the winter months. I've been told the eggs prepared in this fashion remain fresh for up to twelve months!

I've also come across the following preservation procedure in an 1851 County Limerick manuscript receipt book:

10 QUARTS OF WATER

½OZ SALTPETRE

½LB SALT

3 TABLESPOONS OF LIME

Boil water, salt and saltpetre for twenty minutes, then pour the mixture of lime hot. The next day strain off the sediment into another vessel. Let it settle a little again and strain until no sediment is left. Put in the eggs the day they are laid. [13]

CHEESE, CHIVE AND POTATO PANCAKES

One special time of the year when eggs, butter, milk and buttermilk were called into culinary service was the day before Lent began – housewives had to battle to use up surplus stocks of food. The solution lay in the preparation of pancakes, which were the main feature of the Shrove Tuesday night meal. In some areas, the Christmas holly was carefully hoarded and this was used to fuel the fire on which the pancakes were cooked. Sweet pancakes rolled hot with sugar and butter were the usual fare on this night. However, the recipe below is a savoury one, designed to incorporate cheese and a host of other dairy products (see photograph opposite page 75).

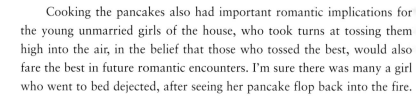

Cooking the pancakes also had important romantic implications for the young unmarried girls of the house, who took turns at tossing them high into the air, in the belief that those who tossed the best, would also fare the best in future romantic encounters. I'm sure there was many a girl who went to bed dejected, after seeing her pancake flop back into the fire.

Makes 24 mini pancakes

½ TEASPOON SALT

2 EGG YOLKS, BEATEN

150ML (5FL OZ) MILK

225G (8OZ) PLAIN FLOUR

25G (1OZ) MELTED BUTTER

175G (6OZ) GRATED RAW POTATOES

50–75G (2–3OZ) GOOD QUALITY CHEDDAR CHEESE, GRATED

1 BUNCH CHIVES, CHOPPED

2 EGG WHITES, WHIPPED

A LITTLE BUTTER FOR FRYING

Mix the salt into the well-beaten egg yolks and add the milk. Sift the flour and add slowly to this mixture along with the melted butter. Mix well. Stir in the grated potatoes and cheese and the chopped chives. Fold in the stiffly beaten egg whites. Pour a little batter into a hot greased frying or griddle pan and cook at once. You can cook about 3 little pancakes at a time. Once bubbles start to break on the surface of each cake, turn and continue to bake until each surface is golden brown.

Serve hot with butter, pickled onions and a little apple sauce (see page 48). They are a perfect accompaniment to Spiced Tongue (see page 34).

GRILLED GOAT'S CHEESE ON A BED OF LEEKS AND TOASTED SODA BREAD

Sheep's and goat's milk, and their respective cheeses, were traditionally

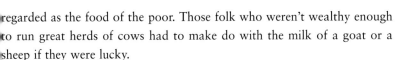

regarded as the food of the poor. Those folk who weren't wealthy enough to run great herds of cows had to make do with the milk of a goat or a sheep if they were lucky.

Serves 4

4 THIN SLICES SODA BREAD (SEE RECIPE ON PAGE 92)

110G (4OZ) SMOKED STREAKY BACON, FINELY CHOPPED

110G (4OZ) LEEKS, THE WHITE PART, SLICED

A LITTLE KNOB OF BUTTER

FRESHLY GROUND BLACK PEPPER

110G (4OZ) GOAT'S CHEESE, THINLY SLICED

Very lightly toast the soda bread slices. Fry the bacon over a moderate heat until crispy. Place the leeks in boiling water, return to the boil and simmer for 1–2 minutes. Strain, add the butter and toss until melted. Season with freshly ground black pepper. Add the leeks to the bacon in the pan and mix well. Spoon the mixture onto the soda bread and top with the goat's cheese. Grill until the cheese has melted and is very slightly browned.

SEAWEEDS

His steed of bacon under him,
With its four hooves of coarse oaten
bread,
With its tail of dulse, from which
seven
Handfuls were pulled every day. [1]

The unpolluted waters off the west coast of Ireland are home to a number of edible seaweeds, three of which have traditionally been favoured by the Irish and welcomed into their diet: dulse, sloke and of course, carragheen moss. It is fair to say that the collection and preparation of seaweeds for the table has been a regional feature of the peasant cuisine, found along the western coastal fringes of Ireland. So much so, that when the French consul, Charles Étienne Coquebert de Montbret, visited West Cork in 1790, he was compelled to comment on the bounty of the sea and the wealth of seaweeds and shellfish:

> *Portions of the rocks at Garretstown stretch out into the sea.*
> *These are covered with plants and marine life such as periwinkles,*
> *called prehán, which are eaten here. Also to be found are the*
> *crab, the lobster, delish [dulse] and slogh [sloke] and a large*
> *species of seaweed with a rod about four or five feet long used by*
> *divers as whips.* [2]

DULSE

Dulse was, and still is, one of the most popularly consumed seaweeds in Ireland that can be picked from the rocks of the middle shore anytime from spring to autumn. Its tough, dark crimson fronds are rich in potassium and mgnesium, and these may be eaten fresh or dried. In either form it makes a popular condiment to accompany oatcakes or potatoes and may also be successfully incorporated into salads and fish dishes. This favourite sea

104

vegetable has an impressive pedigree. The seventh- to eighth-century law-text *Críth Gablach ('Branched Purchase')*, which deals with the status of different individuals in society, stipulates that if a strong farmer calls to your door, he his companion must be entertained with food.

> *He is entitled to the food-provision for two men of milk and curds or corn, butter on Sundays, a sercol of condiments with this, duilesc, onions, salt.* [3]

Later, the twelfth-century Irish text, *Acallam na Senórach (The Conversation of the Old Men)*, pays special attention to the quality of the dulse found in the coves of County Clare, and significantly, today, some of the purest quality dulse comes from this area.

Much of the charm of dulse rests in its versatility as a cooking ingredient. Freshly picked bunches can be fried or stewed with deliciously intense results. For the brave and those with a high salt tolerance, dulse plucked directly from the rocks makes an excellent and healthy chewing gum substitute. Indeed, many a coastal farmer carried a pocketful 'for chewin'', to help him make it through the long working day. Even today, little plastic bags of dulse are a common sight in many seaside pubs.

More often than not, dulse is cut from the rocks at low tide and left to dry on the shingle. Nowadays, the addition of toasted, crispy dulse to a green salad is the ultimate fashion statement! However, for the true dulse connoisseur *creathnach* or shell-dulse is the greatest delicacy of all. This is an exposed shore form of dulse, which is always found in the company of small mussels. Both live together harmoniously on shoreline rocks and outcrops.

To this day, *creathnach* is still a prized delicacy on the Aran Islands, off the west coast of Galway, especially amongst the old people, many of whom comb the shores, risking life and limb, during the summer months, on the lookout for this tasty treat. It is valued predominantly because of its soft and palatable texture.

The recipe which appears on the next page brings together two intrinsically Irish foods; dulse, the produce of the sea and the infamous Irish soda bread.

DULSE SODA SCONES

Makes a baker's dozen

10G (½OZ) DRIED DULSE

450G (1LB) PLAIN WHITE FLOUR

1 TEASPOON BICARBONATE OF SODA (BREAD SODA)

1 TEASPOON SALT

350–375ML (12–13FL OZ) BUTTERMILK

1 EGG, BEATEN

Preheat the oven to 200°C/400°F/gas mark 6, leaving a floured baking tray in the oven to heat.

Soak the dulse in water for 5 minutes. Discard the water and chop the dulse into fine strips. Sieve the flour, bicarbonate of soda and salt into a large cool mixing bowl. Once sieved, run the dry ingredients through your fingers for a few seconds to aerate. Add the chopped dulse. Make a well in the centre and pour in most of the buttermilk. Steadying the bowl with one hand, work in a circular fashion with your other hand to draw the dry ingredients into the milk. Keep working in this fashion until the dough comes together. If you find the dough is a little stiff, then add the remainder of the buttermilk. The dough should feel light and pliable.

On a lightly floured surface, work the dough gently into a round shape, about 2.5cm (1in) thick, with the palm of your hand. Brush lightly with the beaten egg and cut into scones. Place on the heated baking tray and bake in the preheated oven for 20-25 minutes.

Lightly toasted dulse scones are ideal with creamy scrambled eggs.

SLOKE OR SLEABHACÁN

The Welsh were not the only ones to treasure the merits of sloke or sleabhacán (laver), and this delightful seaweed deservedly won immense

popularity in Ireland, taken as a 'kitchen' (a tasty relish) with the ubiquitous potato, or simply boiled and dressed and enjoyed in its own right. The Irish herbalist, John Keogh, refers to dressed sloke in his 1735 work, *Botanalogia Universalis Hibernica (An Irish Herbal)*:

> *when boiled and dressed, it is esteemed by some as a delicate dish.*

and advises in the same breath:

> *it is good against boils and gout.*[4]

But if you should fancy a dish of dressed sloke, it requires a good steady simmering, with constant stirring, for anything up to three hours; by which time you and it are reduced to a pulp. This dedicated cooking meant that sloke was usually served as a supper dish, having spent most of the afternoon on the hearth. But, when dressed with butter and cream and showered with black pepper, piping hot sloke was perfect with oatcakes or mutton. The end certainly justified the means.

CRUASACH

This dish, which can roughly be translated as 'strength' or 'vigour', was a one-time speciality of Inishmurray, a small island off the coast of County Sligo. It was prepared using a mixture of seaweeds boiled together with limpets, and presumably the commonly held belief maintained that anyone who partook of this meal was hardened and nourished for life. I knew little else of the dish until I came across the following piece of advice from the County Galway writer, Séan Mac Giollarnáth, which seemed to refer to a similar dish, but fortunately with more detail.

> *Sloke, shell dulse and ground oats, periwinkles and limpets [were boiled together] and a small drop of the cooking juice was taken with potatoes. There was never a taste like it to be found with any other 'kitchen' (relish). They used to eat the periwinkles and the limpets.* [5]

CARRAGHEEN

Of all the edible seaweeds, carragheen or Irish moss, has a particularly close relationship with Ireland, and it is especially associated with the western coastal regions of the island. Indeed, the name carragheen derives from the Irish word *carraigín*, which means 'little rock', and thus refers to the seaweed's propensity to cling in clusters to the coastal rocks that are washed by North Atlantic waves. Not that carragheen is unique to Ireland; on the contrary, it is to be found throughout the North Atlantic, stretching from the east coast of America to Scandinavia. Despite its widespread distribution, its affinity with the Irish is enduring. Over the generations, this attractive little reddish-purple seaweed permeated the very fabric of Irish rural coastal life. It was valued not only as a foodstuff, but it was also one of the major players in Irish folk medicine. In addition, it was collected, dried and sold, to subsidise the otherwise meagre incomes of the west coast communities.

In the late nineteenth century, the Irish playwright, John Millington Synge, captured in romantic tones the laborious work of the carragheen collectors in County Kerry, on the south-west coast of Ireland:

> *I lay down on the edge of the cliff, where the heathery hill comes to an end and the steep rocks begin. About a mile to the west there was a long headland, 'Feakle Callaigh' [The Witch's Tooth], covered with mists, that blew over me from time to time with a swish of rain, followed by sunshine again. The mountains on the other side of the bay were covered, so I could see nothing but the strip of brilliant sea below me, thronged with girls and men up to their waists in the water, with a hamper in one hand and a stick in the other, gathering the moss, and talking and laughing loudly as they worked.* [6]

Today, the ritual of collecting has much in common with Synge's description. Typically, the delicate branched fronds are plucked from the rocks and rock pools at low tide during the late spring and summer. If the

Opposite: FRAUGHAN SUNDAY CAKE with CREAM (see page 117)

weather holds, the fronds are stretched and spread out on the ground and left to dry and bleach. The end result is firm curls of creamy-brown seaweed, that should be stored in an airtight container, until they are called into culinary service.

The great merit of carragheen, whether fresh or dried, is that it is an excellent source of agar – a sticky gelatinous substance that is used as a thickener and setting agent for both sweet and savoury dishes. Hence in the past, carragheen was popularly used as a milk thickener, when a handful of the moss was simply boiled with a few pints of milk and sweetened with a little sugar or honey. This viscous drink was a popular bedtime beverage, and was consumed in the belief that it was good for sleeplessness. Of course, boiling carragheen with milk is the first rudimentary step in the preparation of carragheen moss blancmange. And alongside carragheen milk, this seems to have been its most popular culinary application. Its use for thickening sweet puddings seems to be referred to by Amhlaoibh Uí Shúileabháin, a schoolteacher and draper from Callan in County Kilkenny, who diligently kept a diary in the early decades of the nineteenth century. In his entry for the 25th of June 1830 he refers to 'second course' or sweet pudding dishes:

> I see a plant like edible seaweed which they call carageen moss. It is largely used by cooks as an ingredient for second course, to give it substance. [7]

Besides its culinary uses, a hot draught of carragheen boiled in water and flavoured with lemon and honey has always been considered an excellent medical standby for coughs and colds. In 1895, Charles R. Browne, a member of the Royal Irish Academy, recorded a more complex cough mixture preparation, common amongst the coastal communities of County Mayo. Here, carragheen was combined with burdock root, broom and furze tops and these were boiled with sugar-stick to make a very effective cough syrup.

Opposite: YELLOWMAN ICE CREAM (see page 121)

109

CARRAGHEEN MOSS BLANCMANGE

Blancmange is a word which instantly stirs up memories of a past era. It is reminiscent of bone china moulds and starched linen. Indeed, the following simple recipe for carragheen pudding is the one that has been used generation after generation and is truly a taste from the past and of all things old-fashioned.

Serves 4–6

7–10G (¼–½OZ) DRIED CARRAGHEEN MOSS (BE CAREFUL NOT TO USE TOO
   MUCH OR YOUR PUDDING WILL HAVE A PRONOUNCED TASTE OF THE SEA)

850ML (1½ PINTS) FULL FAT MILK

A FEW SLIVERS LEMON RIND

2–3 DROPS VANILLA ESSENCE OR A VANILLA POD

1 LARGE EGG

2–3 TABLESPOONS CASTER SUGAR

Soak the carragheen in warm water for 10–15 minutes. (This rejuvenates the moss and releases any trapped sand or tiny pebbles.) Discard the water and place the moss, milk, lemon rind and vanilla in a saucepan. Bring to the boil and simmer for 20–25 minutes over the lowest possible heat. As the mixture simmers gently, it will slowly yet visibly begin to thicken.

Meanwhile, separate the egg and, in a bowl, beat the yolk and sugar together until pale in colour. Pour the milk and carragheen through a sieve onto the sugar and egg yolk mixture; continue beating to ensure that both mixtures are drawn evenly together. Set aside to cool and settle.

Whisk the egg white until stiff and gradually fold in to the carragheen mixture. Place in the refrigerator to set. If you wish to use a mould (to complete the old-fashioned effect) wet the mould so that the pudding is easily released. Serve chilled.

Serving options.
Carragheen Moss Blancmange has a decidedly delicate taste that

110

can be relished on its own or enlivened with the fruity zest of stewed gooseberries or blackberry compote.

Alternatively simply serve with a dribble of honey and Whiskey Cream.

WHISKEY CREAM

150ML (5FL OZ) WHIPPING OR DOUBLE CREAM

2–3 TABLESPOONS IRISH WHISKEY

Lightly whip the cream and stir in the whiskey. If the cream sinks a little after the whiskey is added, whip lightly again for a few seconds to regain its fluffiness.

PEASANT'S JELLY

I have taken this recipe from Florence Irwin's *Irish Country Recipes* of 1937. A County Antrim woman related to her a simple recipe for carragheen jelly. She recounts how the woman gathered a few handfuls of fresh moss to prepare a jelly for her children at suppertime. Firstly, she washed the moss in a stream and placed it in a pot with a few pints of water and 'gave it a good boil'. She then strained it into bowls and, when it had set, the children devoured it cold for supper.

A CURE FOR COUGHS

This was an old reliable in many Irish households used to ward off the inevitable Irish winter coughs and colds. Quick and simple, this velvety drink will soothe a raw throat and calm a harsh cough. Take a good handful of dried carragheen and boil in a pint of water. Add the juice of half a lemon and sugar to taste. To accelerate the curing process, a generous dash of whiskey should be added! [8]

WILD FOODS

Son of fair speckled fruit-clusters
Son of nut-fruit,
son of the tree-fruit. [1]

Some of my earliest memories are of collecting and eating wild foods. My father has spent all of his life working as a professional baker and he would routinely rise at 4am to begin his day's work. His return at lunch time, mindful of an afternoon nap, was very often met with the unreasonable demands of his young daughter, who wished to be taken for a 'spin'. Although weary, he never refused me and would place me on my special seat on the cross-bar of his bicycle and we would set of for an adventure in the countryside. It was from him that I developed my appreciation of nature. I learned the names of wild flowers and birds, I learned to keep blackberries fresh by covering them with fern leaves and I watched in amazement as he baked bread outdoors in a biscuit tin over a primus stove. I particularly remember expeditions to harvest wild strawberries, raspberries, blackberries, watercress, mushrooms, wood sorrel and wild garlic and eating them in the open air: truly an unrivalled culinary experience.

WATERCRESS

Watercress is one of Ireland's wild food treasures, found in great clumps clinging to the banks of fast moving freshwater streams. Throughout the ages, kings, poets, monks and peasants have sung its merits and indulged in its peppery and pungent flavours. Together with brooklime, wood sorrel and wild garlic, it has endured as a favourite salad green, praised in saga and verse.

One of its most famous aficionados was the legendary seventh-century mad king of Dál nAraide – a territory in north Down and south Antrim – Suibhne Geilt, the mad Sweeney, whose story is told in the twelfth-century tale *Buile Suibhne*. Suibhne was a curious character who went mad on the battlefield and fled, literally flew off through the air to engage in a frenzied life of wandering and adventure. Suibhne's path is blighted further, however, when he attempts to expel Rónán Finn, a saint and cleric, from his lands. Restrained by his wife Eorann, Suibhne breaks free from her grip leaving his crimson mantle in her hands and sets out, naked, to attack the cleric, whom he finds in prayer. Suibhne duly seizes his Psalter and flings it in a lake, thereby provoking Ronan to curse his future life and kin, committing him to a life of wandering and flying, naked, throughout the world. Exiled to the wilderness, Suibhne, cold and bare, becomes the archetypal wild man of the woods, surviving on a diet of wild fruits and nuts, and of course bunches of wild cress:

> *My meal is the watercress you pluck,*
> *the meal of a noble, emaciated madman;*
> *cold wind springs around my loins*
> *from the peaks of each mountain.* [2]

But apart from crazy woodmen, watercress also appears to have been a favourite food of the mythical band of heroic warriors, the Fianna. This warrior band, lead by the famous Finn Mac Cumhaill, roamed the Irish landscape engaging in feats of unsurpassed heroic and manly valour, and when it came to food they were very partial to the delights of watercress as they outline in the twelfth-century poem *Acallam na Senórach, (The Conversation of the Old Men)* 'every Beltene we used to consume both the smooth shoots and the head of the watercress'. Elsewhere, they also give details of using fresh watercress and brooklime to garnish plates of cooked wild salmon.

It seems that in the past watercress was mostly consumed as a salad green or taken in sandwiches, wedged between liberally buttered slices of handmade wheaten bread. Indeed, until well into the nineteenth century, wild watercress was offered for sale on the streets of the larger towns and cities. Hard-working women roamed the surrounding countryside gathering up the green plant, and then made their way back to the early morning food markets to sell it. It was always easy to identify the watercress women who hawked their wares barefoot, for shoes were an unnecessary hindrance to them when standing and moving about in the freshwater streams.

Whether it was bought or collected for free, watercress was guaranteed to deliver on flavour, and one of the most engaging references to watercress-eating I know of comes from the pen of William Bulfin, a writer from County Offaly, who cycled throughout Ireland in the early twentieth century, recording his observations at every stop. By the wayside in County Tipperary this is what he saw:

> a man was seated on the grass eating watercress off a cabbage-leaf... Beside the cabbage-leaf, on the grass, lay a piece of brown paper containing a little salt, and he was paying the nicest attention to the quantities which he took with each bunch of cress. 'Is this the Birr Road?' I asked, by way of establishing social relations. He merely shook his head while he dipped a few sprigs of the watercress into the salt and turned the morsel round and round, shaking it daintily, and eyeing it over with the air of an epicure before conveying it to his mouth. [3]

Unfortunately, it is no longer wise to indulge in the pleasures of wild watercress; water pollution coupled with the fear of contracting liver fluke from watercress sprigs that grow near cattle and sheep pasture lands have discouraged people from exploiting this free food resource. If you do want to use watercress as a salad green, it's always best to rely on the shop-bought cultivated variety.

If, however, you intend on cooking wild watercress as a vegetable, or using it for the preparation of soups, then the cooking process eliminates any potential health risks, and of course it's always better fun to gather your food for free. Experienced collectors will tell you that the best sprigs to gather are the older, darker shoots that appear to have a bronzed appearance.

MAD SWEENEY'S WATERCRESS SOUFFLÉ

This recipe is dedicated to the memory of the 'mad Sweeney'. Given his love for the green, he would have savoured this warming and satisfying dish.

Serves 4

225G (8OZ) WATERCRESS (ROUGHLY 2 LARGE BUNCHES)

55G (2OZ) BUTTER

3 TABLESPOONS PLAIN FLOUR

275ML (½ PINT) HOT MILK

SALT AND FRESHLY GROUND BLACK PEPPER

4–5 EGG YOLKS

110G (4OZ) COOLEA CHEESE GRATED, (ALTERNATIVELY, USE A GOOD
  QUALITY GOUDA, GRUYERE OR EMMENTHAL-TYPE)

4–5 EGG WHITES

Preheat the oven to 190°C/375°F/gas mark 5. Leave a baking sheet in the oven to heat.

Wash the watercress very carefully in cold water. It may seem like a large quantity of watercress but don't be put off by the quantity as it will reduce in bulk when it is cooked. Chop the watercress leaves roughly, retaining and chopping some of the stalks for added flavour. Discard the remaining stalks. Put the wet watercress into a large pan (there is no need to add any extra water) and cook over a moderate heat for 5–10 minutes. When the watercress is cooked turn it into a colander and squeeze off any excess liquid. Now melt the butter in a saucepan, add the flour and gradually stir in the milk to make a thick sauce. Add the watercress and season well.

In a food blender, purée the mixture to a smooth consistency. Return to the pan, leave to cool slightly and mix in the egg yolks, one at a time. Blend in three quarters of the cheese and remove from the heat.

Whisk the egg whites until they are stiff and form peaks easily. In a bowl, fold them into the watercress purée with a metal spoon,

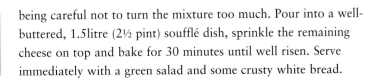

being careful not to turn the mixture too much. Pour into a well-buttered, 1.5litre (2½ pint) soufflé dish, sprinkle the remaining cheese on top and bake for 30 minutes until well risen. Serve immediately with a green salad and some crusty white bread.

FRAUGHANS

The word fraughan or fraochán (meaning bilberry) is derived from the Irish word *fraoch*, which means heather. The small blue berries grow on low-lying scrubs on acidic mountain and bog lands, often concealed amongst the dense growths of heather, where they're ready for picking from late July onwards. It is clear that fraughans have enjoyed a long antiquity in the Irish diet. They feature regularly as favourite wild foodstuffs in early Irish monastic poetry. Similarly, the excavations of Viking Dublin revealed that the berries were savoured by the city's Norsemen in the tenth century. In Ireland, hunting these juicy berries was traditionally associated with the great festival of Lughnasadh, celebrated on the first day of August. Originally this Celtic festival commemorated the deity Lugh, the patron of the arts. Over time and through the influence of the Christian church, this pagan festival, which marked the start of the harvesting season, was moved to the first Sunday in August and became popularly known as Lammas or Garland Sunday.

Fraughan Sunday was considered to be a day of great merriment before the laborious work of the harvest began. Climbing to hill tops, especially to Croagh Patrick, was an established part of the festivities, where picnicking and sport went hand in hand with venerating the local saint. But much more exciting, and possibly pagan in character, was the fact that this Sunday was an annual day of serious and legitimate courting. Much of the courtship rituals were played out in the collecting of the fraughans. Great frolicking and wooing ensued, as anyone who has seen Brian Friel's wonderful play, *Dancing at Lughnasah* will remember.

In some districts, the young bucks showed off their skills to potential partners by skilfully weaving little wicker or rush baskets, which were then presented to the girls for berry picking. Later that evening, the girls would present a fraughan cake to the boys of their fancy at the Fraughan

Sunday bonfire dance (see photograph opposite page 108). Love, sweet cake and dancing must surely be a recipe for successful romance.

FRAUGHAN SUNDAY CAKE

Serves 6–8

175G (6OZ) CASTER SUGAR

175G (6OZ) BUTTER

2 EGGS

225G (8OZ) SELF-RAISING FLOUR

2–3 TABLESPOON MILK

110G (4OZ) BILBERRIES (FRAUGHANS)

Preheat the oven to 180°C/350°F/gas mark 4.

Butter a 18-cm (7-in) round tin. In a bowl, cream the sugar and butter and beat in the eggs one at a time. Sieve the flour into this mixture, adding enough milk to make a stiff mixture.

Fold in the bilberries, making sure they are evenly distributed throughout the mixture. Transfer to the prepared tin and bake for 1 hour. Remove from the tin and leave to cool for 1–2 hours before serving. Serve with Fraughan Cream (see below).

FRAUGHAN CREAM

This is an extraordinarily rich mauve colour.

55G (2OZ) BILBERRIES (FRAUGHANS)

150ML (6FL OZ) WHIPPING CREAM

1 TABLESPOON CASTER SUGAR

In a bowl, mash the fraughans to a juicy pulp. In a separate bowl whip the cream and caster sugar until stiff and add the fraughans. Serve chilled.

This flavoured cream will always make a good accompaniment to summer fruit tarts, pies and fruity ice creams.

SWEETS

Then I saw the door keeper
With his steed of bacon under him,
With its four legs of custard
With its two eyes of honey in
its head. [1]

In rural communities, the fair was the one time for openly indulging in sweetmeats and in all sorts of sweet, sugary delicacies. Apples, gooseberries, plums, gingerbreads, sweet breads and sugar sticks were usual fair delights. Feasting was an accepted and seriously anticipated part of the wider festivities with umpteen food booths and whiskey stalls providing for all tastes. To ensure customer satisfaction, some of the booths even butchered and cooked meat cuts to order, others offered cooked meat pies, salmon, sea-vegetables and shellfish. Of course all of these portable snacks could be enjoyed while sauntering between bric-a-brac, animal pens and the collections of strong young men, restless to make a good bargain as hired farm labourers. The clamour of any Irish fair day is clear from the following list of commodities offered for sale at the Lisburn Fair, County Antrim on the 21st of July 1837:

> *987 horse cattle, 674 black cattle, 587 sheep, 178 pigs, asses,*
> *goats, old clothes, hats, old iron, tin ware, delf and china,*
> *crockery, straw baskets, bee skeps, brooms, toys, bent bottom*
> *chairs, gingerbread, fruit, eels, cockles, cabbages, butter, fowl,*
> *woollen stockings, cheese and dulse.* [2]

Many of the larger Irish fairs were held at times that had once been great Celtic festivals. The days around *Imbolc* (the 1st of February), *Beltene* (the 1st of May), *Lughnasah* (the 1st of August) and *Samhain* (the 1st of November) were

118

noted occasions of social gathering. Others fell in line with Christian Holy Days, such as Easter Monday and St John's Day. But especially popular were the Lammas Fairs held around late July and August, and these were the distant descendants of the two great medieval Lammas fairs; the famous Fair of Tailtean and the Fair of Carman. Both were riotous week-long affairs of bargaining, feasting, matchmaking and merrymaking, hosted by the local aristocracy. One fanciful account of the last Fair of Tailtean in 1168, from the *Annals of the Four Masters*, speaks of a monstrous assembly of people, whose horses and chariots stretched over a distance of six miles causing hazardous street overcrowding and traffic chaos.

Today, one of the last surviving Lammas fairs is held at Ballycastle in County Antrim. This is believed to be one of Ireland's oldest traditional fairs. Its charter dates to 1606, but undoubtedly its origins are of far greater antiquity. Each year, on the last Tuesday of August, sheep and pony dealers bargain the day away, and still amongst the bustling crowds you'll find stalls of hand-made yellowman. Indeed, the 'Oul Lammas Fair' is the real home of yellowman, which is a pale yellow, toffee confectionery, crunchy to the bite and surprisingly bubbly on the tongue. Traditionally, the yellowman makers, who jealously guarded treasured family recipes, arrived at the Lammas fair carrying huge rocks of the pale toffee (popularly known as 'yallaman'), set up their stalls, hammered off golden nuggets of yellowman and packed them into paper cornets for the throngs of children who eagerly handed over their saved pennies. However, for generations it has been particularly associated with young, courting boys who offered it as a love token to soften the affections of their sweethearts, as recalled in a popular traditional ballad 'The Ould Lammas Fair':

> *In Flanders fields afar, when resting from the war,*
> *We drank 'Bon Santé' to the Flemish lassies, oh,*
> *But the scene that haunts my memory is kissing Mary Anne,*
> *Her pouting lips all sticky from eating 'yellowman'.*

> *At the Ould Lammas fair in Ballycastle, oh,*
> *Did you treat your Mary Anne to dulse and yallaman?*
> *At the oul Lammas Fair in Ballycastle, oh.* [3]

YELLOWMAN

Well, if you want to treat yourself to yellowman, the secret of producing a crunchy, honeycombed confection lies in the quantity of bread soda (bicarbonate of soda) used in its preparation. Most traditional recipes call for one level teaspoon of soda to every pound of syrup and half pound of sugar. However, I find that this small amount of soda does not render a very aerated finished product. In the simple recipe below, I've increased the quantity of soda and this produces a wonderfully airy and crisp toffee. Sometimes, recipes also suggest pulling and turning the mixture once it's poured onto a marble slab or greased dish, but this action tends to flatten the bubbly foam caused by the addition of soda, so I prefer simply to pour the mixture and leave it to cool.

Serves 4 (or 2 really greedy people!)
25G (1OZ) BUTTER
1 TABLESPOON WATER
110G (4OZ) BROWN SUGAR
225G (8OZ) GOLDEN SYRUP
1 GOOD TABLESPOON BICARBONATE OF SODA (BREAD SODA)

Melt the butter in a heavy based saucepan over a low heat so that it covers the bottom entirely. Add the water, sugar and syrup and stir until the sugar is dissolved. Turn up the heat and boil steadily, without stirring (a mass of foamy bubbles will be formed), until a few drops of the mixture turn crisp and crackle when dropped in cold water. At this stage, remove from the heat and add the bread soda and stir in well. The mixture will foam greatly at this point and turn pale yellow. Do not be alarmed, it will soon calm down. Pour into a shallow, square greased tin and leave to harden.

Yellowman should keep well for up to a week if stored in an airtight container. It also stores well in the freezer.

YELLOWMAN ICE CREAM

I invented this recipe (see photograph opposite page 109) after I went to freeze some Yellowman and wondered how well it might be combined with ice cream. The ice cream recipe I like best is that created by Myrtle Allen of Ballymaloe House, the undisputed matriarch of food in Ireland, so I have used her recipe as a base with thanks.

Serves 4–6

100G (4OZ) YELLOWMAN *(see recipe above)*

2 TABLESPOONS SUGAR

110ML (4FL OZ) WATER

2 EGG YOLKS

½ TEASPOON VANILLA ESSENCE

570ML (1 PINT) DOUBLE CREAM, WHIPPED

Make the yellowman as outlined above, and when it has cooled break it into 0.5–1cm (¼–½in) squares. Set aside and prepare the ice cream.

In a heavy based saucepan, boil the sugar and water together until it reaches the thin thread stage. (When a metal spoon is dipped into the syrup the last drops will fall from the spoon in long thin threads.)

In a bowl, gradually beat the syrup into the egg yolks. Add the vanilla essence and beat the mixture to a thick white mousse. Fold in the whipped cream and set to freeze.

When it has just set (after about 1 hour) fold in the yellowman and return to the freezer.

This luscious recipe needs no accompaniment.

TOFFEE APPLES

Toffee apples used to be an exciting part of every Irish childhood. Sometimes you'd race into a sweet shop and find, as if by magic, rows and rows of glassy, shiny toffee apples, sitting on their bottoms and staked with wooden lollipop sticks. But if you returned for more the next day, stocks would have mysteriously disappeared, not to seen again for months. Their limited availability was due to the fact that toffee apples were most usually homemade by women, who haphazardly delivered supplies to shops around the larger towns and cities. At other times, gypsy or travelling women would call door to door selling toffee, chocolate and iced apples. Of course, to a child's mind all this uncertainty and sporadic home deliveries only added intrigue to the whole subject and whipped up a great longing for their next appearance.

But as with all cravings, the reality rarely lives up to the dream, and when you finally did get your teeth into a toffee apple, you began to wonder what all the fuss was about, especially when the hard and crispy

toffee shattered, after only one or two bites, leaving you with a sad and bare apple on a stick. With time and reason children worked out for themselves that toffee-apple eating was a swizz that failed to deliver on candy and that was promoted by adults, who saw them as a means of duping candy-starved children into eating fruit.

Nowadays, toffee apples are a rare, if not extinct treat, and so below is a recipe for apples coated in a rich butterscotch toffee.

Serves 4

4 SOFT-FLESHED, CRISP-SKINNED APPLES (COX'S ORANGE PIPPINS ARE GOOD)

4 LOLLIPOP STICKS (IF THESE ARE DIFFICULT TO COME BY, THEN 4 TEASPOONS WILL DO)

For the butterscotch toffee:

450G (1LB) LIGHT BROWN SUGAR

175G (6OZ) BUTTER

2 TABLESPOONS GOLDEN SYRUP

1 TABLESPOON MALT VINEGAR

6 TABLESPOONS COLD WATER

I LEVEL DESSERTSPOON POWDERED CINNAMON

Wash the apples and cut out the stalks. Make a shallow incision across the top of the apples (roughly 1cm/½in long). Push the lollipop sticks right through the core of the apple.

Place the sugar, butter, syrup, vinegar and water in a heavy-based saucepan and stir together over a gentle heat until the butter has melted and the sugar has fully dissolved. Bring to the boil and continue boiling, without stirring, until the mixture reaches 290°C/575°F, or the hard ball stage (i.e. when a little of the mixture is dropped in cold water it forms crisp threads which snap when broken). At this stage remove from the heat and stir in the cinnamon.

Roll the apples in the toffee and ladle more toffee over them to ensure that their entire surface is coated. Sit, top down, on a plate to dry, making sure that the apples aren't touching each other. Once the toffee begins to dry, ladle a little more toffee over each apple to ensure an even coating.

REFERENCES

SOUP & BROTHS

1   MEYER, KUNO. *Aislinge meic Conglinne.* (LONDON, 1892), P34
2   GRAY, ELIZABETH A. (E.D) *Cath Maige Tuired: The Second Battle of Mag Tuired.* IRISH TEXTS SOCIETY (DUBLIN, 1982), P47
3   WOODHAM-SMITH, CECIL. *The Great Hunger. Ireland 1845-1849.* (LONDON, 1991), P179
4   DAY, ANGÉLIQUE. AND McWILLIAMS, PATRICK. (EDS.) *Ordnance Survey Memoirs of Ireland. Vol. Two. Parishes of County Antrim (1) 1838-9.* (DUBLIN, 1990), P9
5   BEHAN, BRENDAN. 'THE CONFIRMATION SUIT', *Brendan Behan's Island.* (LONDON, 1962), P149
6   IRWIN, FLORENCE. *Irish Country Recipes.* (BELFAST, 1937), P12

FISH & SHELLFISH

1   MEYER, KUNO. *Aislinge meic Conglinne.* (LONDON, 1892), P88
2   HUTTON, A. W. (ED.) *Arthur Young, A Tour in Ireland 1776-1779.* VOL I (LONDON, 1892), P37
3   O'MEARA, JOHN J. (ED. TRANS.) *History and Topography of Ireland Giraldus, Cambrensis.* (PORTLAOISE, 1982), P37
4   ANONYMOUS. 'A TOUR IN IRELAND 1672-4'. CONTRIBUTED WITH NOTES BY JAMES BUCKLEY. *Journal of the Cork Historical and Archeological Society.* VOL. X (CORK, 1904), P88
5   ANONYMOUS. 'LETTERS FROM THE COAST OF CLARE' *Dublin University Magazine.* MARCH–SEPTEMBER. VOLS. XVII &XVIII (DUBLIN, 1841), P349
6   McGRATH, THE REVEREND MICHAEL. (ED. & TRANS.) Cinniae Ambhlaoibh Uí Shúileabháin. *The Irish Texts Society.* vols. XXX–XXXIII

(LONDON, 1936), PART III, P35
7   MAXWELL. WILLIAM HAMILTON, *Wild Sports of the West of Ireland.* (DUBLIN, 1892), P140
8   ESTYN E. EVANS. *In county Kerry one man would hold another under water...* IRISH FOLKWAYS (LONDON, 1957), P230
9   THACKERAY, WILLIAM MAKEPEACE. *The Irish Sketch Book, 1842.* (LONDON, 1865), P26
10 STOKES, GEORGE T. (ED.) *Pococke's Tour of Ireland in 1752.* (DUBLIN, 1891), P37
11 EDWARD, ARNOLD. (ED.) THE REVEREND S. HOLE REYNOLDS, *A Little Tour in Ireland by an Oxonian.* (LONDON, 1892), P158
12 MAXWELL, WILLIAM HAMILTON. *Wild Sports of the West of Ireland.* (DUBLIN, 1892), P140

BEEF

1   MEYER, KUNO. *Aislinge meic Conglinne.* (LONDON, 1892), P78
2   MAC AIRT, SÉAN. & MAC NIOCAILL, GEARÓID. (EDS.) *The Annals of Ulster.* PART I (DUBLIN, 1983), P469
3   LUCAS, A.T. 'IRISH FOOD BEFORE THE POTATO' *Gwerin 3.* 1960
4   BINCHY, D. A. (ED.) *Corpus Iuris Hibernici.* (DUBLIN, 1978) P480
5   BEST, R. I. AND BERGIN, OSBORNE. (EDS.) 'FLED BRICREND'. *Lebor na Huidre* (DUBLIN, 1992), P248 21-23 ANCIENT LAWS OF IRELAND (DUBLIN, 1865-1901) P239 14-19
6   BEST, R. I. 'THE SETTLING OF THE MANOR OF TARA' *Ériu IV.* (DUBLIN, 1910), P125
7   MORYSON, FYNES. *Itinerary.* (1617) QUOTED IN CONSTANTIA MAXWELL'S *Irish History from Contemporary Sources (1509–1610).* (LONDON, 1923) P313.
8   CAMPION, EDMUND. *Two Bokes of the History of Ireland.* (1570)

QUOTED IN MYERS, P. (ED.)
ELIZABTHAN IRELAND. *A Selection
of Writings by Elizabethan Writers.*
(CONNECTICUT, 1983), P28
9 KELLY, JAMES. (ED.) *The
Letters of the Lord Chief
Baron Edward Willes to the
Earl of Warwick, 1757–1762*
(ABERYSTWYTH, 1990), P49
10 DEPARTMENT OF AGRICULTURE,
Cookery Notes. (DUBLIN, 1936)
11 *Bunreacht na hÉireann* THE
IRISH CONSTITUTION
(GOVERNMENT PUBLICATIONS
OFFICE, DUBLIN, 1936), P136
12 IBID. ARTICLE 41.2.2, P138
13 BENNET, J. A. W. AND SMITHERS,
G. V. (EDS.) 'THE LAND OF
COKAYGNE' *Early Middle
English Verse and Prose.*
(OXFORD, 1968), P21

LAMB & MUTTON
1 MEYER, KUNO. *Aislinge meic
Conglinne.* (LONDON, 1892), P78
2 CARBERRY, MARY. *The Farm by
Lough Gur.* (CORK, 1973), P233-34
3 STOKES, GEORGE T. (ED.)
*Pococke's Tour of Ireland in
1752.* (DUBLIN, 1891), P92
4 MYERS, JAMES P. (ED.) GERNON,
LUKE. 'A DISCOURSE OF IRELAND
1620' *Elizabethan Ireland,*
(CONNECTICUT, 1983)
5 MACLYSAGHT, EDWARD.
*Irish Life in the Seventeenth
Century.* (DUBLIN, 1939), P342
6 MAXWELL. WILLIAM HAMILTON,
Wild Sports of the West of Ireland.
(HAMPSHIRE, 1986)
7 ANONYMOUS. 'LETTERS FROM THE
COAST OF CLARE – NOS. VIII AND
IX' *Dublin University Magazine.*
NO. CV. SEPTEMBER, VOL. XVIII
(1841), P366
8 PERSONAL COMMUNICATION: ROY
SHIPPERBOTTOM.
(FOOD HISTORIAN) YORK, ENGLAND.

PORK
1 MEYER, KUNO. *Aislinge meic
Conglinne.* (LONDON, 1892), P88
2 KEANE, JOHN B. *Strong Tea.*
(CORK, 1963), P72
3 THURNEYSEN SCELA, RUDOLF. *Mucce
meic Datho.* (DUBLIN, 1935), P2
4 MURPHY, DENIS (ED.) *The Annals
of Clonmacnoise.* (DUBLIN,
1896), P176
5 BINCHY, D. A. (ED.) *Corpus Iuris
Hibernici.* (DUBLIN, 1978),
P480: 23-26. ANCIENT LAWS OF
IRELAND (DUBLIN, 1865-1901)
P239 19-24
6 EDWARD, ARNOLD (ED.) THE
REVEREND S. HOLE REYNOLDS, *A
Little Tour in Ireland by an
Oxulan.* (LONDON, 1892)
7 WOLLASTON HUTTON, ARTHUR.
(ED.) *Arthur Young's Tour in
Ireland 1776–1779.* (LONDON,
1892), VOL II
8 PERSONAL COMMUNICATION:
CATHERINE BUCKLEY (1994)
9 MEYER, KUNO. *Aislinge meic
Conglinne.* (LONDON, 1892), P60-62

POULTRY & GAME
1 MEYER, KUNO. *Aislinge meic
Conglinne.* (LONDON, 1892), P84
2 BUCKLEY, J. 'A TOUR IN IRELAND IN
1672–4' *Journal of the Cork
Historical and Archaelogical
Society.* VOL 10 1904
3 BINCHY, D. A. (ED.) *Corpus Iuiris
Hibernici.* (DUBLIN), 1978, P73.
21-27 ANCIENT LAWS OF IRELAND
(DUBLIN 1865-1901), P117. 23-30)
4 THACKERAY, WILLIAM
MAKEPEACE. *The Irish Sketch
Book 1842* (LONDON, 1865), P179-80
5 WOLLASTON HUTTON, ARTHUR.
(ED.) *Arthur Young's Tour in
Ireland 1776–1779.* (LONDON,
1892), VOL II, P49-50
6 MCGRATH, M. (ED.) 'CINNLAE
AMHLAOIBH UÍ SHUILEABHÁIN (THE
DIARY OF HUMPHRET O'SULLIVAN'),
(LONDON, 1892)
7 Ó CUIV, B (ED.) 'THE ROMANCE
OF MIS AND DUBH RIS' *Celtica* 2.
(1954)

FRUIT & VEGETABLES

1   MEYER, KUNO. *Aislinge meic Conglinne.* (LONDON, 1892)
2   KINSELLA, THOMAS. (ED.) *The Tain.* (OXFORD, 1989)
3   NELSON, CHARLES, E. *This Garden to Adorne with all Varietie. The Garden plants of Ireland in the centuries before 1700.* MOOREA 9 1990, P40
4   IBID.
5   IBID.
6   WOLLASTON HUTTON, ARTHUR. (ED.) *Arthur Young's Tour in Ireland 1776–1779.* (LONDON, 1892), VOL 11
7   MCGRATH, THE REVEREND MICHAEL. (ED. & TRANS.) 'CINNLLAE AMHLAOIBH UI SHUILEABHAIN' *Irish Texts Society, Vols XXX–XXXIII* (LONDON, 1936), PART 1, P95
8   COSGRAVE, H.A. 'THE IRISH CHANNEL AND DUBLIN IN 1735'. *Journal of the Royal Society of Antiquaries of Ireland.* VOL IX (1899), PART 1 P59
9   POPULAR SONG
10 MRS DREW. *Receipt Book.* 1801 (MOCOLLOP CASTLE, BALLYDUFF, CO. WATERFORD). BY KIND PERMISSION OF DIANA SANDES OF FLOWER HILL, BALLYDUFF, CO.WATERFORD.

POTATOES

1   ROEDER, CHARLES. *Notes on food and Drink in Lancashire and other Northern Counties.* PART 2. PETITS PROPOS CULINAIRES 42 (1992), P36
2   WOLLASTON HUTTON, ARTHUR. (ED.) *Arthur Young's Tour in Ireland 1776–1779.* (LONDON, 1892), VOL 1. P238
3   POOR INQUIRY (IRELAND) FIRST REPORT FROM HIS MAJESTY'S COMMISSIONERS FOR ENQUIRING INTO THE CONDITION OF THE POORER CLASSES IN IRELAND WITH APPENDIX (E) AND SUPPLEMENT

British Parliamentary Papers XXXII (LONDON, 1836), P2
4   LARKIN, EMMET. (ED. & TRANS) *Alexis de Tocqueville's Journey in Ireland July–August 1835.* (DUBLIN 1990), P29
5   POOR INQUIRY (IRELAND) FIRST REPORT FROM HIS MAJESTY'S COMMISSIONERS FOR ENQUIRING INTO THE CONDITION OF THE POORER CLASSES IN IRELAND WITH APPENDIX (E) AND SUPPLEMENT. *British Parliamentary Papers 1836 XXXII,* P1
6   MCGRATH, THE REVEREND MICHAEL. (ED. & TRANS.) 'CINNLAE AMHLAOIBH UÍ SHÚILEABHÁIN.' IRISH TEXTS SOCIETY VOLS XXX–XXXIII (LONDON, 1936). PART 11, P317
7   WILDE, WILLIAM. 'THE FOOD OF THE IRISH' *Dublin University Magazine.* VOL XLIII, P131
8   REID, THOMAS. *Travels in Ireland.* (LONDON, 1823), P203
9   WILDE, WILLIAM. 'THE FOOD OF THE IRISH' *Dublin University Magazine.* VOL XLIII, P128
10 IBID. P133
11 POPULAR FOLK SONG
12 IRWIN, FLORENCE. *Irish Country Recipes.* (BELFAST, 1937), P81
13 WILDE, WILLIAM. 'THE FOOD OF THE IRISH' *Dublin University Magazine.* VOL XLIII, P132

CEREALS

1   MEYER, KUNO. *Aislinge meic Conglinne.* (LONDON, 1892), P78
2   FYNES, MORYSON. *Itinerary* 1617. P193. QUOTED IN MYERS, P. (ED.) *Elizabethan Ireland. A Selection of writings by Elizabethan Writers.* (CONNECTICUT, 1983) P186.
3   SOMERVILLE LARGE, P. *The Irish Country House.* (LONDON, 1995)
4   JOYCE P.W. *A Social History of Ancient Ireland.* (DUBLIN, 1907) P141
5   GWYNNE, E. J. 'RULE OF THE CÉLI DÉ' *Hermathena* 44 2ND SUPP. VOL. (1927)

6   GWYNNE, E. J. 'THE TEACHING OF
    MÀEL RUAIN' *Hermathena* 44
    2ND SUPP. VOL. (1927)
7   MACLYSAGHT, EDWARD. *Irish Life
    in the Seventeenth Century.*
    (DUBLIN, 1939), P337
8   IBID. P345
9   SHANE LEHANE: PERSONAL
    COMMUNICATION
10 RECORDS IN THE IRISH FOLKLORE
    COMMISSION ARCHIVE

EGGS & DAIRY PRODUCE

1   MEYER, KUNO. *Aislinge meic
    Conglinne.* (LONDON, 1892), P36
2   O MUIMHNEACHAIN, AINDRIAS.
    (ED. AND TRANS.) *Stories from the
    Tailor.* (CORK, 1978), P28
3   MEYER, KUNO. *Aislinge meic
    Conglinne.* (LONDON, 1892), P100
4   MURRAY, THE REVEREND ROBERT
    H. (ED.) *The Journal of John
    Stevens 1689–1691.* (OXFORD,
    1912), P139
5   MORYSON, FYNES. *Itinerary.*
    (1617) QUOTED BY MYERS, P.
    (ED.) *Elizabethan Ireland. A
    Selection of writings by
    Elizabethan Writers.*
    (CONNECTICUT, 1983), P190
6   BOLLANDISTS. (ED.) *Acta
    Sanctorum.*VOL 4 (PARIS, 1863), P158
7   CLANCY, PATRICK. ET AL *Ireland:
    A Sociological Profile.*(DUBLIN,
    1986), P162
8   MORYSON, FYNES. *Itinerary.*
    1617. QUOTED BY MYERS, P.
    (ED.) *Elizabethan Ireland. A
    Selection of writings by
    Elizabethan Writers.*
    (CONNECTICUT, 1983), P190
9   KNOTT, ELEANOR. *Togail Bruidne
    Da Derga.* (DUBLIN, 1975), P16
10 MEYER, KUNO. *Aislinge
    meic Conglinne.* (LONDON,
    1892), P84 AND 68
11 IBID.
12 MACLYSAGHT, EDWARD. *Irish Life
    in the Seventeenth Century.*
    (DUBLIN, 1939), P337-38
13 ELIZA HELINA ODELL'S RECIPE

BOOK AUGUST 1851. BY KIND
PERMISSION OF HELEN ALLOTT,
BALLINGARRY, CO. LIMERICK

SEAWEED

1   MEYER, KUNO. *Aislinge meic
    Conglinne.* (LONDON, 1892), P88
2   'A FRENCHMAN'S IMPRESSIONS OF
    COUNTY CORK IN 1790' *Journal
    of the Cork Historical and
    Archaeological Society.* LXXIV
    (1974), PART 1, P14
3   BINCHY, D.A. CRÍTH GABLACH.
    (DUBLIN, 1979), P138
4   SCOTT, MICHAEL. (ED.) *An Irish
    Herbal Botanalogia Universalis
    Hibernica 1735.* (DUBLIN,
    1991), P138
5   RECORDS IN THE IRISH FOLKLORE
    COMMISSION ARCHIVE. *Mac
    Giollarnàth, Séan. Annàla beaga
    ò Iorrus Aithneach* (DUBLIN,
    1941), P270, (AUTHOR'S TRANSLATION).
6   SYNGE J.M. *Wicklow, West Kerry
    and Connemara* (DUBLIN, 1980), P91
7   MCGRATH, THE REVEREND
    MICHEAL. (ED. & TRANS.) '
    'CINNLAE AMHLAOIBH UÍ
    SHÚILEABHÁIN *The Irish Texts
    Society'* vols XXX–XXXIII
    (LONDON, 1936), PART 11, P291

WILD FOODS

1   MEYER, KUNO. *Aislinge meic
    Conglinne* (LONDON, 1892), P32
2   O'KEEFE, J. G. (ED.) 'THE
    ADVENTURES OF SUIBHNE GEILT'
    The Irish Text Society. VOL XII
    (DUBLIN, 1996), P89
3   BULFIN, WILLIAM. *Rambles in
    Eirinn* (DUBLIN, 1907), P13

SWEETS

1   MEYER, KUNO. *Aislinge meic
    Conglinne.* (LONDON, 1892), P88
2   DAY, ANGÉLIQUE. AND MCWILLIAMS,
    PATRICKH. (EDS.) *Ordnance Survey
    Memoirs of Ireland.* vol 8 *Parishes of
    County* ANTRIM (II) 1832–8
    (DUBLIN, 1991), P74
3   BALLAD OF THE OULD LAMMAS
    FAIR

FURTHER READING

ALLEN, DARINA. *Irish Traditional Cooking* (London 1995)

CULLEN, LOUIS. *The Emergence of Modern Ireland* (London 1981)

IRWIN, FLORENCE. *Irish Country Recipes* (Belfast, 1937)

LAVERTY, MAURA. *Never No More*. (London 1942)

LUCAS, A'T. 'Irish Food Before the Potato', *Gwerin iii*

MAHON, BRÍD. *Land of Milk and Honey*. (Dublin 1991)

LIST OF RECIPES